ARTISTS'
INTERIORS

ROCKPORT

GLOUCESTER MASSACHUSETTS

ROCKPORT
PUBLISHERS

ARTISTS'
INTERIORS

CREATIVE SPACES, INSPIRED LIVING

LAURIE E. DICKSON

First published in the United States of America by
Rockport Publishers, Inc.
33 Commercial Street
Gloucester, Massachusetts 01930-5089
Telephone: (978) 282-9590
Fax: (978) 283-2742
www.rockpub.com

Library of Congress Cataloging-in-Publication Data
Dickson, Laurie.
    Artists' interiors : creative spaces, inspired living / Laurie
Dickson.
        p.   cm.
    ISBN 1-56496-952-5 (hardcover)
    1. Artists—Homes and haunts. 2. Interior decoration—History—20th
century. I. Title.
NK2115.3.A78D53 2003
747—dc21   2003008832
                                            CIP

ISBN 1-56496-952-5

10 9 8 7 6 5 4 3 2 1

Design: Yee Design
Copyeditor: Pamela Elizian
Proofreader: Stacey Ann Follin

Printed in China

CONTENTS

INTRODUCTION

My home in the mountains is my sanctuary. I feel blessed to have created a life where I can work from home in a place I love. The Rocky Mountains called to me at an early age. John Denver's "Rocky Mountain High" drifting through my teenage bedroom in rural New York inspired me to head West. The stunning beauty, dramatic landscapes, and majestic presence of the mountains continue to move me somewhere deep inside. Though I've had more homes than I can count, my spiritual home lies within the blue skies, wide-open spaces, and breathtaking vistas of the San Juans, the San Miguels, and the La Plata Mountains. No matter where I've landed, the home I create and the surrounding environment have been essential to my well-being. My heart is where my home is.

  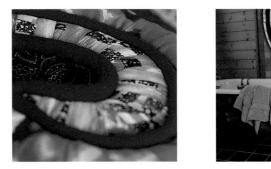

My mother designed my childhood home. My father supported her, and her talent for design blossomed in their dream home. Frank Lloyd Wright was her first architectural inspiration; his influence was clearly reflected in our flat-roofed, contemporary house built into a hill. It stood out from the many '50s-style tract homes that were indicative of the times. Style, art, music, and architecture were integral parts of my upbringing. My career as an architectural photographer for magazines is a direct result of those early influences and my mom's encouragement.

In all my travels to various homes and gardens, the homes of artists have exhibited the richest textures, the most unusual colors, and the most memorable personalities. These dwellings break all the rules, yet, at the same time, apply them with perfection. The spaces these artists inhabit mirror their vivid interior lives. Full of objects and treasures that reveal beauty and humor—or intentionally sparse and free from clutter to allow more room for quiet contemplation—their rooms are as unique as their art. Their lives and habitats are so eccentric they seem to float outside the trends pushed by decorating magazines. Sometimes an artist's style speaks so loudly that the general public can't relate. Other times, it's so quiet the

are their canvases as much as the paint and clay are the materials with which they compose. In each of their lives art, home, work, and beauty are inseparable. They are my friends, mentors, and teachers whose lives are nurtured by their surroundings. That is what moved me to photograph these sacred domains.

style seems reminiscent of times gone by. The artist homes on these pages are all of the above. Sarah's in Mousehole, Cornwall, is as it sounds—small as a mouse hole. Eberhard's is expansive—a renovated military hospital. Meeting and spending time with these artists has been a journey that has broadened my vision and inspired me to live with a deeper commitment to my own home and life. They make me want to live artfully, playfully, thoughtfully, and more colorfully. These homes and studios

Artists are the inventors of original style. They are the trendsetters, the boundary breakers, and the creative souls who look within to find the inspiration for styling the environment that embodies their vision and nourishes their lives. I hope the sharing of these lives and sanctuaries will delight and encourage you to explore your own artistic interiors, within and beyond, as they have encouraged me.

THINKING BIG FIEBIG

∧ THIS SCULPTURE GRACES THE CENTER OF THE CAMPUS AT THE
UNIVERSITY OF KASSEL, GERMANY.

< EBERHARD FIEBIG DEMONSTRATES HIS TECHNIQUE
OF "PYROGRAPHY."

> EBERHARD AND DOROTHEA HAVE CREATED A NEUTRAL PALETTE
TO SERVE AS A BACKDROP FOR THEIR PAINTINGS. THE SOFT
TEXTURES OF WICKER COMPLEMENT EBERHARD'S ANGULAR
SCULPTURES.

Eberhard and Dorothea bought an old military hospital that was built during World War II. The large brick structure allows them to enjoy space that is rare by European standards. The building is softened by the surrounding sculpture gardens and deck. They transformed the four floors into a spare, contemporary environment where they live and work. With the addition of a simple kitchen and wooden floors and the removal of some walls, they created an enviable living and working/gallery space.

Eberhard is a published author, photographer, sculptor, and, as one reporter succinctly put it, "Germany's best-known unknown artist." His monumental sculptures grace many public places throughout Europe and invite the viewer to enter his world. His hard-angled arches represent the feminine and masculine and mimic the folding and unfolding that occurs in nature. His country home gives him the opportunity to experience nature up close. Much of our conversation focuses on nature and its importance to his work. Eberhard believes that, "If we see art, we see nature in our own way." Dorothea hasn't given up the city yet and still maintains a busy schedule between their home in the country and Frankfurt, where she teaches, works, and shows her paintings.

Both Eberhard and Dorothea have a strong sense of aesthetics, as is evident in their extensive bodies of work and the thoughtful design of their home. Simple furnishings, white walls, warm wooden floors, and soft, flowing curtains provide a perfect backdrop and gallerylike setting for showing their art. The luxury of a generous space allows

> (top left) EBERHARD'S FAVORITE DINING AND ENTERTAINING SPOT, HIS DECK, IS READY FOR AFTERNOON TEA.

> (bottom left) THE SPARSE, WHITE KITCHEN HAS A PANEL OF GLASS AS A BACKSPLASH.

> (far right) THE LIBRARY HOUSES A GRAND COLLECTION OF BOOKS ON ART, POETRY, AND PHILOSOPHY.

them to separate their workspace from their living environment. Each enjoys an entire level as a studio. Eberhard's workspace requires printers, tables, and six computers as well as machinery for making models and room to paint. He also has an entire library to house photographs he has published over the years.

Their home is essential to their work, functioning as a blank canvas that beckons them to create. Little attention and focus are given to the actual backdrop that is their home. Instead, their work and ideas emerge as a result of the thoughtful design of the space, the country setting, and the room to keep making very big art.

∧ THE FORMER MILITARY HOSPITAL, WHICH WAS TURNED INTO A RESIDENCE, IS SURROUNDED BY SCULPTURE GARDENS.

> (top, bottom left) THE OPEN, AIRY LIVING AND DINING AREA ALSO SERVES AS THE PERFECT GALLERY FOR EBERHARD'S SCULPTURES AND DOROTHEA'S PAINTINGS. SOFT, SHEER CURTAINS DIFFUSE THE LIGHT FROM THE WINDOWED WALL. SPARSE BUT THOUGHTFUL FURNISHINGS ADD ELEGANCE.

> (bottom right) THIS SHELF IS FILLED WITH EBERHARD'S MODELS FOR HIS SCULPTURES.

➡ *Eberhard quotes the German poet, Rilke, "If you see art that moves you, you have to change your life." After two wonderful days of philosophizing and exploring the art and intriguing life that Eberhard lives, my life has changed. I've been moved by his devotion to his art and beliefs. We ate and drank and struggled through our German and English, laughing all the way, but somehow the passion he has for where he lives, his love for Dorothea, and the art he creates needs no translation.*

LIVING OUT LOUD

^ HAPPY ARTIST KATHLEEN PEARSON SITS IN HER ART CAR, "HEX MEX,"
SEEMINGLY IMMERSED IN A SEA OF DASHBOARD ART, WEARING CLOTHES
THAT SHE DESIGNED. (SHE ALSO LOVES TO COLLECT BUTTONS.)

> THE ART CAR "HEX MEX" SITS IN FRONT OF KATHLEEN'S STUDIO IN
BISBEE, ARIZONA. SEEING A DESERT SUNSET REFLECTED IN THE WIN-
DOWS, THE GLOW OF THE ICE CREAM CONE TOPPING THE CAR, AND THE
WINDMILLS SPINNING, ONE CAN EASILY IMAGINE THE ATTENTION SHE
GETS DRIVING THROUGH THE STREETS OF BISBEE. KATHLEEN WAS RAISED
IN A PENNSYLVANIA STEEL TOWN SURROUNDED BY MANY PENNSYLVANIA
DUTCH FARMS, FAMOUS FOR THE HEX SIGNS PAINTED ON THE BARNS.
WITH A NOD TO HER PAST, SHE USED THE HEX SIGNS AS A STARTING
POINT FOR HER DESIGN AND LOOKS TO HER PRESENT LOCATION IN
ARIZONA, JUST A FEW MILES FROM THE MEXICAN BORDER, FOR
OBJECTS THAT COMPLETE THE "MEX" PORTION OF HER CONCEPT.

➥ I'm enjoying a quiet breakfast in the quaint mining town of Bisbee, Arizona. Looking out the window, I glimpse the most spectacular car driving by. It's covered with stuff—everything, including the kitchen sink—and topped with an ice cream cone.

I'm committed to finding this car and the person behind the wheel. It's not hard in a town the size of Bisbee, and, sure enough, I soon run into her on a bench in front of her parked car. The car is hard to miss, and Kathleen is exactly who I imagined would be driving it.

∧ A FAVORITE VINTAGE LAMP, ACQUIRED THROUGH A TRADE, ACCENTS THE WILD MIX OF COMFORTABLE CHAIRS IN THE LIVING ROOM.

> (opposite) KATHLEEN'S COMIC AND COLORFUL COLLECTIONS RANGE FROM CARTOON CHARACTERS TO SUMO WRESTLER DOLLS AND GAUDY RELIGIOUS ICONS. THE NEON LIGHT, DESIGNED BY A FRIEND, ADDS ANOTHER PLAYFUL ACCENT TO THE ROOM.

Kathleen Pearson's art cars have made her famous in town and beyond. They have been part of her world since 1990. She is unfazed by the attention they attract. The cars are her art and her life, and she's proud of all the work that goes into their design. She has had over a hundred shows of her work, including exhibitions of her cars. A happily married mom and grandmother, Kathleen travels frequently to show one of her three cars. She writes poetry, designs clothing, and paints. She calls her paintings "pop folk art" and uses many familiar icons from contemporary culture as models and themes. The paintings are bright, funny, and provocative. It is not a surprise to see Kathleen's trademark style—which draws from kitsch culture—dominating her home overlooking Bisbee.

➥ *If you don't like bright color and lots of stuff, you may not like Kathleen's home. But once you get to know her, it's hard to resist the charm of it all. Kathleen is comfortable with Kathleen, and her big heart quickly won me over. She is generous and thoughtful in all her endeavors.*

➦ As we meet for the final sunset shot of Kathleen's car at her studio, a crowd of friends has gathered. There is another art car artist who has arrived for a visit as well as a handful of her fans. A tourist couple walks up and starts photographing her car as we all watch. There is never a dull moment for this local celebrity who thrives in this small community. The desert glow is descending, pink clouds are reflected in the window of the light green adobe building, the ice cream cone gleams on the top of the car as we finish the last shot—a fantastic ending to a fanciful day.

Kathleen loves her things, arranging collections, creating vignettes, and designing altars. Surrounding herself with the things she loves inspires her to create—the more the merrier. In her fabric designs, she isn't afraid to use a wild animal print next to a bold plaid. Designing clothes with her bargain fabrics comes naturally.

"I'm drawn to certain styles, especially from the '40s, '50s, and '60s." She has collected antiques and vintage furnishings all of her adult life. She may trade a piece of art for a lamp or make a special dinner in exchange for a table. Kathleen is as creative with her methods of collecting as she is with incorporating them into her home. She will obsess about collecting particular things. For example, her "postcard" room is the result of 20 years of gathering those images; the dashboard of her "Hex Mex" car came from years of collecting brooches.

Kathleen sees little separation between her art and all other aspects of her life. She drives her art and wears her designs. Her advice for developing your own style: "Have faith in your own creativity, and don't pay any attention to what people may say. Criticism is not a positive aspect of art." She thinks positive reinforcement and being true to yourself are key when it comes to developing your own style. It is important not to take the lazy way out. If you don't have the money, then go to thrift stores and yard sales. "I believe in having faith in yourself—that's why I have it tattooed on my arm." She laughs, "The day my art car, 'Love 23,' and I were made into refrigerator magnets, I felt I had made it, that I had reached my goal as a successful pop icon artist."

> KATHLEEN'S PAINTINGS SET THE MOOD FOR THE DINING ROOM AND WORK PERFECTLY WITH THE '60S DINETTE SET. ALL THE TRIM AND DOORS HAVE DIFFERENT, BRIGHT PAINT COLORS.

∨ (pages 22 and 23) THE "POSTCARD" ROOM ABOVE HER STUDIO OFTEN SERVES AS A LANDING PLACE FOR GUESTS. KATHLEEN LOVES SITTING IN THE ROOM AND FEELS IT GIVES HER PEACE—UNDERSTANDABLY, AFTER 20 YEARS OF COLLECTING OVER 4,000 IMAGES AND THE HOURS IT TOOK TO PASTE THEM UP.

HARBOR HIDEAWAY

I must go down to the sea again, to the lovely sea and sky

And all I ask is a tall ship and a star to steer her by.

And all I ask is a windy day with the white clouds flying

And the flying spray and the blown spume

And the seagulls crying.

Taken from a poem by John Masefield that artist Sarah Grierson-Irving painted around the ceiling of her living room.

< JUST STEPS AWAY ON SARAH'S STREET, SHE ENJOYS HER BELOVED VIEW OF THE HARBOR IN MOUSEHOLE.

> BOATS ARE THE INSPIRATION FOR SARAH'S LITTLE COTTAGE. FROM FOUND ART ABOUT BOATS TO FABRICS THAT CARRY FORWARD THE NAUTICAL THEME, SHE CLEVERLY REFLECTS THE HARBOR INSIDE HER HOME.

Sarah Grierson-Irving is an extraordinary woman. Her life embodies freedom of a kind that most can only glimpse, even though she experiences difficult physical limitations. She generously welcomes anyone who may wander down the narrow alley of her Cornish village into her home. Mousehole is a tiny English fishing village surrounding a picturesque harbor. A more appropriate name for the town and Sarah's cottage would be hard to find. Covering a total of maybe 500 square feet (46.5 square meters), Sarah has carefully filled every corner. Boats, books, gardening, and her art are her passions, all of which are at the center of her decorating. When she retired from teaching, she quickly transformed the dark wood and stone into a painted, colorful, and cozy retreat that reflects the harbor scenes she so dearly loves.

Sarah's art is her life now. Although her doctors often try to turn her attention to the problem of having Parkinson's disease, she spends little time worrying about her limitations. She knows her healing is in her art. She collects what the sea leaves behind and makes simple, usually boat-themed collages to sell in the local galleries. Photography, painting, and gardening are talents she has mastered. From her *trompe l'oeil* painting in the alley garden to the painted seascapes that grace the walls of her home, she has transformed mundane rooms into extraordinary spaces. She captures the harbor scenes with her camera and creates greeting cards. She has found a way to live the life she loves in the area that is so dear to her.

> THE NARROW ALLEY THAT LEADS TO SARAH'S HOUSE IS NOT WIDE ENOUGH FOR A VEHICLE, BUT IT IS BIG ENOUGH FOR THE CROWDS THAT GATHER TO ADMIRE HER GARDEN. SHE CULTIVATES THE LUSH HAVEN IN POTS, BOAT HULLS, AND ANY OTHER VESSEL THAT HOLDS DIRT.

< SARAH'S TALENTS SHINE IN HER *TROMPE L'OEIL* PAINTING OF PITCHERS AND DRIFTWOOD ON HER ALLEY WALL, BECKONING THE OBSERVANT PASSERBY TO LOOK AGAIN.

26

^ (top) EVEN SARAH'S CAT, MOLLY, HAS A SPECIAL CORNER, COMPLETE WITH HER OWN MENU.

^ (bottom) SARAH'S CORNISH DISHWARE STANDS OUT AGAINST THE COLORFUL GREEN WALLS AND HER BRIGHT YELLOW TOASTER.

On the wall, handwritten: *I must go down to the sea again to the lonely sea and the sky*

She claims she has "always been able to make a home out of a tea chest." Her two-story retreat is barely as big as a tea chest but larger than life when it comes to creative innovation. From the curtain rods made of boat oars to the bedsprings-turned-candleholders to the old boat-hull-turned-garden-container, she sees potential in the "treasures" the sea leaves behind. She has always remodeled her homes and gathered ideas from garden and home decorating magazines. She knows that everybody can do something original with his or her living environment. Her advice is "not to look at your space as it is, but as you'd like it to be." Her approach is that she decorates a small area and makes a picture out of it. Then she looks at another area and makes a picture out of it. Each corner of her cottage is just that—a perfect picture. Sarah lives on a modest income, so she understands how to be frugal. She recommends buying white paint and adding your own tints, creating your own palette. She is firm when the teacher in her says, "Never copy anybody else because it shows a singular lack of character."

Mousehole is the place Sarah has dreamed about since she was a child. She will no doubt spend the rest of her days there. The townspeople watch out for her, often bringing her their own finds from the sea for her creations. Her love of the sea and all its treasures are what inspire her to keep moving, even on the challenging days.

➥ My days with Sarah are a gentle reminder of hope and appreciation for the small things. She has made a life from so little, facing challenges that would stop most of us, but she perseveres with grace and dignity. When I'm faced with someone who claims he or she couldn't do something creative or inspired in their homes because of a lack of money or resources, I will always think of Sarah. There is a poem Sarah painted on the risers of her stairs that ascend to her living quarters, and it reminds me of the delicate gift of life:

"I have spread my dreams under your feet Tread softly because you tread on my dreams."

—W.B. Yeats

JAZZY PARISIAN PAINTER

< FRANÇOISE BIVER IN HER STUDIO.

> THE OPEN FLOOR PLAN OF FRANÇOISE'S AND
YVES'S PARISIAN FLAT IS WARMED BY PERSIAN RUGS
AND COLORFUL FABRICS. THE CLEAR STORY OF
WINDOWS AROUND THE KITCHEN AND THE SKY-
LIGHTS PROVIDE A LIGHT AND AIRY ATMOSPHERE IN
ALL AREAS OF THE HOME.

∨ SMART STORAGE UP THE STAIRS MAXIMIZES SPACE.

My dear Parisian friend, Antonia, is leading me to her neighbor's home. "Très jolie!" is how she describes what I'll find behind the old warehouse walls. But then Antonia is always saying, "Très jolie"—and when she is especially moved, "Oo la la!"—so I am convinced that what I'm about to see is something special. Françoise ushers us into her home while I quickly reach for my French-English dictionary. Although our conversation is halting, Françoise has a quiet, easy nature and immediately makes me feel welcome.

Françoise Biver and Yves Dormay have an enviable Parisian property. Centrally located in the up-and-coming Canal District of Paris, they have transformed a 100-year-old leather warehouse into an artists' sanctuary. It's a piece of the country tucked quietly away in the heart of the city. Embracing the ease and comfort of a country home, the flat also portrays cosmopolitan sensibilities. In addition, Françoise and Yves have the uncommon luxury in Paris of a garden courtyard entry.

Françoise and Yves bought the old building with another couple and divided it into separate living spaces. Françoise needed a roomy painting studio, and Yves, who is a commercial airline pilot and a professional jazz musician, wanted recording space. The solution to the relatively open floor plan meant two separate lofts on either end of the flat to accommodate their working environments. Much of the decor is simple and understated with music being central to their living area. Living, dining, and office spaces share the center of the home. Many recycled materials were used throughout the home, including the windows that wrap the kitchen, the wood that makes up of much of the trim and stairs, and the large beams that run the length of the flat. Françoise loves the country feeling they've created at home but wouldn't trade her city living for anything. Access to music and clubs is essential because Yves often performs his eclectic jazz there, whereas the art scene with its galleries and openings is central to Françoise's routine. Françoise also spends a good deal of her time volunteering with special-needs children several days a week in the city.

^ PERSIAN RUGS, A COZY COUCH, AND PILLOWS WITH AN INDIAN FLAVOR PROVIDE THE LIVING ROOM SEATING.

< THE KITCHEN IS SMALL AND SIMPLE, SURROUNDED BY RECYCLED GLASS WALLS. CABINETS ARE WORN AND REUSED, AS IS THE METAL DOOR OFFSET BY CONTEMPORARY PENDANT LIGHTING. EXPOSING AND PRESERVING THE RAW BEGINNINGS OF THE BUILDINGS AS WELL AS USING RECYCLED MATERIALS THROUGHOUT ARE ALL PART OF THE DESIGN THEME.

Francoise's paintings reflect her visual affinity for all things country, from the rhythmic paintings of garden-fresh vegetables to the rolling landscapes of her imagination. She starts with drawings of a selection of vegetables from the local market and develops a still life for her paintings from there. Her delicate but defined physical presence is good metaphor for her unique style of oil painting as well. Sensuous forms move across her canvases, repeating, but never the same. Her painting loft is filled to the ceiling with the vegetable studies. The oil landscapes dancing across the walls reflect an organic quality similar to the rhythm in the vegetables. The light that fills her studio through the diffused skylights that run the length of the home are primary to Francoise's successful working conditions. Yves's studio is a private, custom-designed work area that accommodates his recording equipment and musical instruments.

∧ FRANÇOISE HAS THE IDEAL PAINTER'S LOFT. HER
  VEGETABLE STILL-LIFE PAINTINGS AND LANDSCAPES
  COVER THE WALL FROM FLOOR TO CEILING, GIVING
  A PERSPECTIVE OF THE VOLUME OF HER WORK.

< YVES'S MUSIC STUDIO OCCUPIES A LOFT AT ONE
  END OF THE FLAT.

ARTISTS' INTERIORS

DIVINE DUMPSTER DECOR

^ PORTRAIT OF NANCY SCOTT AT A SHOW OF HER PAINT-
INGS IN BISBEE, ARIZONA.

< THE GRACIOUS WARMTH OF THE SCOTT'S ENTRY INVITES
YOU FARTHER INTO THE HOME.

> THE EARLY MORNING LIGHT IN THE SUNROOM IS FIL-
TERED THROUGH THE BARGAIN BAMBOO SHADES. THE
COMFORTABLE CHAISE LOUNGE PILED WITH PILLOWS
FOR A SUNNY READING SPOT. THE THRIFT STORE ELE-
PHANT TAKES ON A NEW LOOK WITH A FRESH COAT OF
PAINT. IRON TABLES SHOW OFF NANCY'S MOSAIC WORK.

Nancy Scott could tell you the best days to comb the alley dumpsters in all the towns in which she has lived. Bisbee, Arizona, feels like it may be the town in which she and her husband Larry will retire, but believing this is the last house she'll remodel would take a lot of convincing for anyone who knows her. After only a couple of years of living in this quirky desert mining town, she already is known as "Nickel Nancy." Finding bargains and scavenging yard sales, she has an enviable ability to make something of nothing—and not just *something*, but something beautiful. As a painter, Nancy transforms the mundane, often-painful side of life into whimsical stories on canvas. She feels her art is a part of all she does at home, and although she doesn't show her paintings in the formal setting of her house, the paintings are exhibited in local galleries.

When Nancy and Larry found this house, it wasn't the most interesting architecturally, but it had the right amount of floor space and studio room for her so they would "not be bumping into each other." Nancy explains, "This house was so ugly, but I knew the bare bones of the house were good. This house needed me. It was all of the kinds of things I knew I could change. The house wanted me." They fell in love with the town and the people and didn't want to live in a community that was "full of a bunch of other old duffers." The home and what it eventually became under Nancy's golden touch is all part of her art. Transforming a house is often the art that satisfies her, and she considers that her art as much as her painting. Nancy believes that the design of a home begins within the individual. She says, "With all that's wrong in the world, it's important to make one place right—the nest where you dwell. To me the greatest satisfaction is being surrounded by the things you love, the things that bring you joy."

➻ I know some of the colorful and difficult stories of her past, so it's easy to see how her dedication to her surroundings and the collections that fill it are important to her. There is a compulsive side to her need to beautify and change, but it is her discerning eye and artistic impulse that turn someone else's trash into her own delightful treasures. There is not a house that she doesn't like and wouldn't like to get her hands on, which is why believing this house is her last is like believing I'll never want to eat ice cream again!

< THE ART OF ARRANGING COMES NATURALLY TO NANCY. HER COLLECTION OF POTTERY SHINES IN THIS SETTING OF BOOKS, PRINTS, AND *OBJETS D'ART*. EVEN HER PANTRY IS AN ELEGANT SHOWCASE.

An elegant sense of design and color is evident in Nancy's and Larry's home. Nancy has style, and, in this case, style comes cheap. She looks for things that go with other elements she already has in place, or, in the case of a new room, sometimes just one unique piece will set the tone. An old couch takes on new life with a bargain fabric slipcover she has made. Many of the collections she has in this house came with her from their last house, but they have an entirely different look with fresh colors and slight alterations. Her Asian-influenced collections are a new direction that she effortlessly combines with her older collection of '30s pottery and rustic country furniture.

Nancy knows that there is a connection between herself and her environment. Every collectible is noticed daily, triggering the fond memory of its acquisition or the circumstances around its discovery. Peaceful surroundings and harmony in her environment are imperative. From her first days with Larry in a 10 foot x 15 foot (3 m x 4.5 m) trailer ("It was darling!") to the Mediterranean desert villa they now call home, her fearless approach to decorating knows no home it can't transform into a little piece of paradise. "It doesn't take a lot of money. It takes patience to shop around, to look for bargains, and to know that making a room come together doesn't just happen all at once. If you love something, then you can find a way to make it work. It's also about being able to do something creative every single day. It gives a sense of value and validation to my life to explore my own creativity."

> (top) NANCY'S CHOICE OF A NEUTRAL BACKDROP ADDS TO THE DRAMA IN HER LIVING ROOM. RICH ANIMAL PRINTS, VELVETS, AND SHEER CURTAINS GIVE THE AIR OF ELEGANCE, YET MOST OF THE DECOR IS SALVAGED, REFURBISHED, OR OTHERWISE RESCUED FROM A PREVIOUSLY DULL LIFE.

> (bottom) NANCY LOVES OLD BLACK-AND-WHITE PHOTOS AND PRINTS AND DISPLAYS THEM NEXT TO HER MORE RECENT COLLECTING PASSION—ORIENTAL POTTERY. THE LAMP WAS MADE FROM AN OLD DOWEL SHE PAINTED AND A BARGAIN VINTAGE FIXTURE. LUCKILY, LARRY IS HANDY WITH WIRING.

SAN FRANCISCO CHIC

< PORTRAIT OF SILVIA POLOTO WITH HUSBAND BILL AND SON LIAM.

> STRONG COLOR, CONTEMPORARY ACCENTS, UNCLUTTERED LIVING, AND STRIKING PAINTINGS ARE THE KEY ELEMENTS OF SILVIA AND BILL'S LOFT IN SAN FRANCISCO. STARTING WITH THE FOUNDATION OF THE NATURAL CARPETS FROM BILL'S GALLERY, THE CAREFULLY CHOSEN PIECES OF FURNITURE, AND SILVIA'S PAINTINGS THAT FILL THE APART-MENT, THEIR HOME IS A LESSON IN DESIGN.

^ SILVIA'S PAINTINGS LINE THE ENTRY HALL.

OLD CHURCH PEWS PROVIDE THE PERFECT DINING ROOM
SEATING IN A ROOM GRACED BY ONE OF SILVIA'S LARGE,
HORIZONTAL PAINTINGS. THE SMALLER CAFÉ TABLE
AND CHAIRS ARE A PLAYFUL AND LIGHTER SCULPTURAL
JUXTAPOSITION TO THE FORMAL DINING.

This loft in San Francisco was about light—light and space. Silvia and Bill had looked for quite a while before they found the downtown location. The space provided Silvia opportunities with her art she hadn't previously had. With no space or storage limitations, this loft gave her the room to work big. The environment has been critical to the development of her art. Luckily, she and Bill wanted the same things in their living space. Silvia loves color and loves to mix styles—antiques with contemporary lighting, bright colors with classic furniture. Bill has a natural affinity for designing interiors and operates a fine gallery of natural woven rugs. When she and Bill began their search for a place that could accommodate her studio and their growing family, they saw this loft and knew they had found home. Silvia's connection to their home is visible everywhere you turn. It really is a gallery for showing her paintings and sculptures, and she frequently invites potential buyers to view her work there. Lacking many of the "standard" features of an ordinary home, such as windows or a floor plan, that are typical of other apartments, they have never felt that the home is lacking. Quite the contrary, they love the daylight from their many skylights and the privacy of the layout.

→ Silvia's enthusiasm and excitement are palpable when I speak to her about my book featuring artists' homes. She knows her home is the ideal candidate for the book and isn't afraid to say so. Her energy is infectious, so I'm equally excited to see how she has transformed the former bakery into a hip dwelling in San Francisco. Many worlds meet in the home of artist Silvia Poloto, her husband Bill McDonnell, and their son Liam. She's a lively, dark-haired beauty from Brazil and met her Irish husband in São Paulo, Brazil. They made the move to San Francisco about 10 years ago. The conversation dances between Portuguese and English with a thick Irish accent, and I'm struck by the diversity in their lives as well as the rich mix and contrasts they've achieved in their loft.

Silvia's inspirations for her paintings are from within. She likes working in series and looks to all kinds of sources for her inspiration, including books she has read and images she has dreamed, but mostly she is inspired from within. She has studied art at San Francisco City College but is really a self-taught and very successful artist. Relatively new to the scene, she has devoted her life to sculpture and painting and has many galleries that show and sell her work. An engineer by training, when she moved to the United States, she began a new life as an artist and has never looked back. "Everybody should be able to do what they like. They think they must do whatever they can to make ends meet, and it's so sad. I would be miserable if I were still doing engineering."

Silvia's dwelling is a big part of her art. The home that she and Bill inhabit is a direct reflection of her large, abstract painting and sculpture. They work together, forming their look from the hand-loomed rugs that Bill imports, the antiques that speak to them at auctions, and the paintings that grace the walls. She knows that her house is a mirror for her work and the perfect place to exhibit.

∧ SILVIA'S STUDIO AND LIAM'S PLAY SPACE.

< SILVIA'S LARGE, METAL SCULPTURES GREET VISITORS
   IN THE COMMON AREA OF HER BUILDING.

PEACEFUL SANTA FE PUEBLO

< ESTELLA LORETTO IN HER GARDEN WITH HER SCULPTURE OF A DEER HUNTER ENTITLED *REAWAKENING*.

> THE WARM LIGHT SPREADS ACROSS THE LIVING ROOM. HAND-CARVED LOGS AND CORBELS FRAME THE STRUCTURE THROUGHOUT.

∨ ESTELLA'S BRONZE OF *MORNING PRAYER* LOOKS TOWARD THE RISING SUN. THE LITTLE WINDOWS IN THE ENTRY OF THE HOUSE REPRESENT STARS TO NATIVE AMERICANS AND ARE ESTELLA'S TRADEMARK SYMBOL.

⚫ Perched on a mesa above the twinkling lights of Santa Fe is the pueblo-style home of artist Estella Loretto and her daughter Fawn. From this high desert haven the sun setting in the Western sky is an enduring glow of crimson that only New Mexico skies can produce. No home evokes the feminine spirit as much as the sensuous curves and colors of Estella's soft, pink adobe, and no one embodies the feminine spirit quite like Estella. She has a presence. She is graceful, gentle, and powerful all at once.

Estella Loretto makes deliberate choices and is rarely swayed from achieving what she sets out to accomplish. Moving softly through the diverse and elegant art world of Santa Fe, clad in velvet and lace and always with the finest jewelry of her own design and making, you know you are in the presence of greatness, and if you don't know, she may have to gently remind you. Her smile and charm engage you, and her audience is always captive.

Born and raised in the Pueblo of Jemez, New Mexico, Estella is a Towa-speaking Native American, one of about 4,000 left today. Her unusual path to fame as a prominent Native American woman sculptor began at her pueblo, took her around the world, and has brought her once again to her homeland in New Mexico. "Most people don't leave the village. Our culture is still very much alive and full of ceremony and tradition, but I always had a desire beyond the pueblo. I had an adventurous spirit and wanted to travel." A family friend gave Estella a subscription to *National Geographic*, and from the age of 12, she started mapping the world and the places she wanted to see.

> ESTELLA'S STUDIO IS DWARFED BY THE WORK IN PROGRESS—*PRAYER FOR PEACE*, A 9/11-INSPIRED SCULPTURE.

< ESTELLA OFTEN HAS HER SISTER GLENDA HELP WITH DETAILS. THIS PIECE IS A SMALLER VERSION, TO BE CAST IN BRONZE, OF THE NATIVE AMERICAN SAINT, KATERI TEKAKWITHA. IT WILL STAND IN FRONT OF SANTA FE'S LARGE HISTORICAL CATHEDRAL NEAR THE PLAZA.

Estella's studies and travels include the Institute of American Indian Arts in Santa Fe and the prestigious Oomato School of Traditional Japanese Art. After much globe-trotting, she left Japan to return to her home and family in Jemez. She studied the traditions of the pueblo potters from her mother and grandmother. Her primary teacher and renowned sculptor, Allan Houser, was the person most responsible for inspiring her to do monumental sculpture. She began focusing her energy on her sculpture and ran her own gallery on Canyon Road, Santa Fe's famous gallery district. In addition, Estella had the challenge of balancing her career and raising her daughter. Estella comments, "It's so beautiful to see her grow up. I don't want my work ever to be more important than the time I spend with her, but my sculptures are my children, too."

As Estella's story unfolds, I realize that her power came from following a path, a dream set forth as a child, sticking to that path with unwavering certainty, and having faith and trust that life is unfolding perfectly. Her actions and choices are a reflection of these principles. On the day I told Estella about my book, long before it was a reality, she encouraged me to "follow what is in your heart and it will happen."

Estella's home was an inspired move. When she found the land to build on, the floor plan came naturally. "I like things to flow and move easily. I didn't want any sharp angles and would often instruct the contractor to add more curves." She called on friends Christine and Jeffrey Crozier to help with the delicate addition of a soft wash of colors and *trompe l'oeil* touches. Morning glories climb the walls and birds fly in their make-believe world—all feminine touches that distinguish her style.

Upon the completion of her home and studio, Estella closed her gallery of 10 years and began operating solely from her home studio. Estella's adobe home is full of her sculptures, paintings, and pottery. The home has become a showcase for her work. Her living room windows look out on her garden, full of her sculptures.

The house embodies the pueblo style of architecture. It is a living sculpture that suits Estella perfectly and embraces her traditional culture. Today she is grateful for the experiences her travels and other cultures gave her. "They made me appreciate who I am, where I came from, and that I am a Pueblo woman. I really and truly believe that by doing monumental sculpture, by following my dreams and listening to my intuition, I will be shown the right path. I am making this dream happen. My images and sculpture will take care of me."

Her art and her home speak to the pueblo life. Her monumental pieces are at home in many private collections, as well as in the entry of the state Capitol building in Santa Fe and the Albuquerque Museum in Albuquerque, New Mexico. The Institute of American Indian Arts is home to the deer hunter sculpture *Reawakening*, coming full circle to Estella's beginnings in the world of art.

^ ESTELLA'S SOFT, FEMININE TOUCH IS EVIDENT EVERY-WHERE. THE KITCHEN HAS A GRACEFUL ARCH OF ROSES HAND-PAINTED ON THE WALLS. HER NATIVE AMERICAN POT COLLECTION FRAMES THE WINDOW. THE DINING AREA ADJOINS THE KITCHEN.

< ESTELLA'S DAUGHTER FAWN IS THE SUBJECT AND MODEL FOR THIS SCULPTURE, ENTITLED *MAGICAL ENCOUNTER*. FRAMED WITH MORNING GLORIES AND ONE OF ESTELLA'S PAINTINGS, EVERY CORNER EXHIBITS ART. FRIENDS AND ARTISTS CHRISTINE AND JEFFREY CROZIER CREATED THE *TROMPE L'OEIL* SCENES THROUGHOUT THE HOUSE. HUMMINGBIRDS, MORNING GLORIES, AND THE ROSE ARCH IN THE KITCHEN ARE ALL PART OF THE FANCIFUL SCENES THEY CREATED.

ARTISTS' INTERIORS

FOREST ROOMS

^ MARY ELLEN LONG AND HER DOG IN THE WOODS NEAR HER HOUSE.

> (this page) THE LONG'S COMFORTABLE LIVING AREA IS FILLED WITH ETHNIC COLLECTIONS FROM THEIR TRAVELS, AS WELL AS MARY ELLEN'S ART. THE TALL, HANDMADE PAPER CYLINDERS ARE ACTUALLY PART OF AN INSTALLATION OF CAST SCULPTURES FROM HER ASPEN FOREST.

> (opposite) THIS IS THE VIEW THAT GREETS YOU UPON ENTERING MARY ELLEN AND WENDELL'S HOME. THE TALL WINDOWS REACH TO THE SECOND FLOOR AND OPEN TO THE OUTSIDE.

Mary Ellen Long and her husband Wendell built their home outside of Durango, Colorado, 20 years ago. They wanted a place that would incorporate her studio into their home, and they accomplished that by placing the studio at the center of the house. It is the core of the structure, the epicenter of activity. No one embodies an artist's sense of place as much as Mary Ellen. Her work is from and about place. The materials she gathers, the site where she displays her work, and her studio in which she creates it are here. The location, at 8,500 feet (2,591 m) above sea level, played a significant role in bringing Mary Ellen's art closer to the raw wilderness and the outdoors, which is her canvas and medium at the same time. The dramatic change of seasons, the surrounding wildlife, and the forest fire that nearly destroyed their home have had a powerful influence on her direction.

Mary Ellen's work is hard to peg and often the hardest to photograph, yet the profound manipulations of the landscape leave the viewer with a sense of reverence and an appreciation for nature as art. Her art involves the tradition of working in a sculptural way, subtly intervening with nature, which differs from landscaping or gardening. Aspen forests and ponderosa pines surround Mary Ellen's and Wendell's home, and contained within are a system of paths and what she calls "Forest Rooms." Each room is a different, quiet place, such as the *Forest Library*, where decaying, old books are placed in a spiral, slowly melding with the earth, or the *Oak Maze Room*, where oak branches have been arched and joined to form a sculptural maze. When asked about the inspiration for these rooms, Mary

> (opposite, bottom) THE SECOND-FLOOR BUNKROOM IS A FAVORITE RETREAT FOR GRANDCHILDREN.

> (opposite, top) THE HOT TUB SITS IN A CENTRAL LOCATION IN THE LIVING ROOM WHERE MARY ELLEN AND WENDELL CAN ENJOY OUTSIDE VIEWS AND WARMTH FROM THE LIVING ROOM FIREPLACE.

> (opposite, far) A BONE CURTAIN CONSTRUCTION, WHICH MOVES IN THE WIND, HANGS OUTSIDE THE HOME.

My friends are at home in these secluded woods. Fires have threatened them, snow impedes their travel, and drought has distressed the wildlife. In the end it all becomes material for future art projects. There is a blurring of where the inside of the house begins and the outside rooms start. The studio and home gently nestle into the landscape, and the aspen forest warmly embraces Mary Ellen's delicate additions.

➵ *My mom and I headed to visit Mary Ellen and Wendell for my last photo shoot. Although the road to their home was a little scary on this wintry day, it only added to my mom's admiration for Mary Ellen. I watched as she explored little books and boxes and was taken by all the fascinating objects and nature-inspired art in their home. The very effect that Mary Ellen hopes to achieve with visitors was accomplished with my mom. She still talks of that day, Mary Ellen's striking art, its relationship to their place, and what makes their home so special. Her art is about honoring a place while observing and gently manipulating the natural world. A visit to this earthen sanctuary and a walk in her woods is a delightful window into her art and an unexpected angle on nature.*

> (this page and opposite, top) MARY ELLEN DESIGNED THE HOME SO THAT HER STUDIO IS CENTRALLY LOCATED. HER WORK AND HER RETREAT IN THE HOME ARE ONE AND THE SAME.

> (opposite, bottom) COLLECTING EVERYTHING, FROM BONES TO TWIGS AND BARK, INVOLVES STORAGE. MARY ELLEN DEVELOPED STORAGE THAT IS ORGANIZED AND BLENDS WELL WITH THE NATURAL DECOR. MANY OF THESE ELEMENTS BECOME THE MATERIAL FOR HER HANDMADE PAPERS.

Ellen says, "All animals do this. I watch the ones in my forest, gathering for winter or collecting things for their nests. I used to feel I was intruding, but now I have only respect for the place and my part in it. I am part of a movement of art that works with the landscape in a nontraditional way. The landscape manipulations bring art to everyone in a way that galleries and paintings sometimes don't."

Mary Ellen and Wendell have created a home that nurtures her work as an artist and their life together and is architecturally interesting. Their work with local architect Dean Brookie helped achieve all of their unique requirements. There are high windows and vaulted ceilings to create a spacious feeling. The multiple levels with oddly shaped rooms all make for a home that is functional, private, and open to the wooded surroundings.

Their Japanese-style hot tub area is centrally located. They can enjoy the stars, a cozy fire, and a warm soak—all in the comfort of their living room. The design choices were all carefully planned, knowing the kind of space required for Mary Ellen's work. Wendell always jokes, "Just call me Mr. Mary Ellen." Their place is often home to Mary Ellen's classes, paper-making workshops for interested art patrons. Mary Ellen says, "I want a visitor to feel comfortable to explore and to ask questions—to be curious enough to open a box lid and discover the art within. The light of the interior allows them to see the transparent forms and textures in my art and collections."

Mary Ellen's work continues to transform and grow from inside her house to outside in the forest. Recent fires that came close to home became the raw material for new work. Mary Ellen's art mirrors the changes in the world around her, and the home where she works continues to support her inspirations.

WEST PALM PARADISE

< PORTRAIT OF BRUCE HELANDER IN HIS WEST PALM BEACH STUDIO.

> THE ENTRANCE TO THE HELANDER'S HOME HAS A DISTINCTLY OLD-WORLD FEELING. THE RELIGIOUS ICONS, UPON CLOSER LOOK, HAVE A BIT OF HUMOR. THE ENSHRINED STATUE IS THE "DELTA BATTERY MAN," A FLEA-MARKET FIND.

∨ THE LIVING ROOM IS AN INTERESTING JUXTAPOSITION OF COLONIAL STYLE AND COLLECTIBLE KITSCH.

It's an unseasonably hot day for October in West Palm Beach, but coming from the cool north I expected hot and sultry in Florida. An unexpected treasure is what lies behind the dense tropical canopy that surrounds Bruce Helander's old Mediterranean-style compound. Bruce considers his collage work to be like visual crossword puzzles. His home is also a bit like a crossword puzzle. Kitschy objects fill the house and raise questions about their origins and meanings. Even with all these varied collections, the home lacks clutter, and the eclectic pieces of the puzzle fit together with style.

When Bruce Helander comes home from his day at the studio, he doesn't want his home to be an exception to his artistic endeavors; he wants it to be a visual extension. He feels that his home is a marriage of his vision of his art and his life with his wife, Claudia. She enjoys putting their home together just as much as he, and their mutual love of foraging flea markets provides them with an endless decorating resource. They want to reflect warmth, wit, and eccentricity with things that keep them visually stimulated in their home. Collecting is their passion. Bruce explains, "Every artist should collect something. If you have vision, a discriminating eye, and something that interests you, then why not collect? The more the merrier; the more the common denominator increases the value of all that you have—like having lots of soldiers in different uniforms, but they're all marching to the same tune." Bruce's friend, glass artist Dale Chihuly, got him interested in flea markets when he was at the Rhode Island School of Design. The Boston area proved to be ripe with flea markets, and Bruce began his first collection. "My idea is, when I come home I want the same feeling of excitement that I have with my art. My home is my castle, and if you're an artist, the objects that surround you must be perfect—perfect outsider art, perfect folk art, perfect advertising art—but perfect in their imperfections, and they must meet your sensibilities. Claudia and I are avid collectors of Americana, but it's really whatever moves us."

Bruce comes to this place in his life with an enviable résumé of art and design experience. He graduated from Rhode Island School of Design (RISD) with a master's degree in fine arts. He later became dean of the college at RISD, acquiring atypical organization and

> (opposite, top and bottom) BRUCE'S LARGE ACRYLIC PAINTING, *TRELLIS TRAINING (WITH CLOCK)*, IN THE LIVING ROOM, ABUTS THE DOOR TO THE VERANDA OUTSIDE. CLAUDIA SPENDS MANY HOURS PLANTING AND TENDING THE GARDENS. THE VERANDA PROVIDES A YEAR-ROUND LIVING AREA.

> (opposite, far right) THE DINING ROOM IS A SHOWCASE FOR ADDITIONAL COLLECTIONS, INCLUDING THE VARIETY OF CITRUS HAPPY FACES, POP-CULTURE ICONS OF THE SUNSHINE STATE.

➡ *Bruce and I end our day in his studio. There is a lot going on, with his two assistants organizing projects and scheduling. His numerous creative endeavors are spread about, including the magazine article he's writing on Yoko Ono and his latest art pieces. There are boxes and stacks of the raw material for his collages everywhere. The prominent West Palm Beach address is just a small bit of evidence of the success Bruce has achieved. He's happy in his work, he's madly in love with his wife, and his art continues to thrive. His infectious enthusiasm and devil-may-care approach to style and art have been a cornerstone for his success. As we prepare for his portrait, he grabs a frame and smiles. With the afternoon sun providing the light and his easy manner in front of the camera, the portrait is a breeze, and the flea-market frame is the perfect element to contain the many aspects of Bruce Helander.*

business skills while at the same time keeping in touch with the art world. In 1981, he started and sold the magazine *Art Express*, then headed south and hasn't looked back. He opened successful galleries in Palm Beach and New York City, representing artists such as Robert Rauschenberg, Jules Olitski, John Chamberlain, and James Rosenquist. All the while he continued his late-night work in his studio, assembling, cutting, and pasting his trademark collage art. In 1995, he took a calculated leap, got out of the gallery business, and devoted his life to his own art. His list of clients and collectors is testimony to his wise decision. They include the *New Yorker*, the United Nations, the Washington Opera, the Boston Film Festival, the Palm Beach International Film Festival, and many private and public collections. "After hanging pictures every day or advising clients how to live with art, you develop a certain sensibility about placement. The one mistake people make when they put their house together is worrying 'What will people think?'—and we could care less!" Bruce and Claudia collect with a discerning eye, and they have no interest in a resale value so the otherwise worthless, authorless objects may have just as much value to them. It's all about the design and the

original spirit. Of course, when they were looking for the perfect imperfect house, they had some requirements. The home had to be old, have high ceilings, be close to Palm Beach, and be in an interesting neighborhood. In the five years since they moved, Claudia's green thumb has generated a veritable jungle of orchids, palms, and ferns. They added Mexican-tile floors, a new roof, and updated plumbing and electrical systems. Their priority was to find a house with a wonderful spirit, and the work involved to bring it up to date is part of the package. The art, the antiques, and collectibles all fit gracefully into the confines of their house.

Bruce believes that everyone has his or her own vision. By creating an environment where you really want to get up in the morning, make a cup of coffee, and enjoy the surroundings, you'll have a better day. Bruce says, "By getting in touch with your spirit, not caring what other people think, and dancing to your own tune, your life is richer in terms of visual harmony. The elements that tie together in your home, wardrobe, and garden, or the meals you cook all become richer because of your inner vision."

∧ THE DINING ROOM IS A SHOWCASE FOR ADDITIONAL COLLECTIONS.

< (opposite) THE KITCHEN IS NO EXCEPTION TO FOUND, USED, OR SECONDHAND STYLE.

MANHATTAN VIEWS
IN VIBRANT HUES

^ PORTRAIT OF APRYL MILLER AND HER DAUGHTERS, DYLAN ON THE LEFT AND
LYRIS IN THE CENTER.

> (center) THE DEN AREA IS A COZY NICHE THAT FEATURES VENETIAN PLASTER IN
A RAINBOW OF COLORS ON THE WALLS AND CEILING. THE CARPET IS A LOOMED
DESIGN.

> (far right) EVEN THE HALLS AND CLOSETS ARE A COLORFUL DISPLAY. THE APART-
MENT ENCOMPASSES THE ENTIRE 29TH FLOOR, WITH ROOMS LEADING OFF FROM
THE ENCIRCLING HALLWAY.

If you want to get jewelry designer, collage artist, and furniture designer Apryl Miller excited, just talk about matching things or color coordination. Those are fighting words in her book, and her haven is a reflection of all the ways that things don't match up. Juxtapose color and pattern, with more going right next to it, and you have some of the basic ingredients of how this 4,000-square-foot (372-square-meter) apartment comes together. Clashing is the rule, and the final product is one of sublime excitement.

Apryl breaks rules. From working with her architect—she asked him to forget about doing anything like what he'd done before—to working with the plasterers, she always pushed them a little further than they'd gone before. Each room has a plethora of textures and surfaces, and over a hundred different colors of latex paint were used throughout the apartment. She painted grout because she couldn't find colors bright enough, and painted glass to create the tiles on her countertops. She dug her fingers into the plaster surface that became the design on her bathroom wall. Beads, found plastic objects, and Pollack-like splashes of paint were all part of her design.

Apryl explains, "The building, design, and final product that is my home is not about making anyone but me happy ." She says, "Even though people may be timid about what to do in their homes and how to do it, there are many things people could do that would have a lot of meaning to them and make their space more personal." For example, Apryl points out the ray of sun design in her daughter

> (opposite, top and bottom left) APRYL'S COLLECTION OF VINTAGE FURNITURE HAS A NEW LIFE UNDER HER ARTISTIC HAND. THE COUCH WAS REDESIGNED AND COVERED WITH VARIOUS '70S FABRICS. TWO OF APRYL'S COLLAGES HANG IN THE CORNER.

> (opposite, bottom right) APRYL CALLS THIS ROOM HER CHAIR FACTORY. FULL OF CHAIRS THAT WILL EVENTUALLY BE WORKS OF ART, THIS ROOM IS A CATCHALL AND INCLUDES THE FABULOUS VIEW OF NEW YORK CITY.

69

➥ *We're dressing up for a night on the town. I feel like a country mouse in the big city, especially when Apryl appears in her evening attire. She dons a thrift-store, bright-green, camouflage-print skirt; a large, pink belt that I know would look cheap on me; a blue and lavender Oriental-style blouse; huge platform sandals; and a multitude of bracelets and bangles. She looks dazzling, and I scramble for any color I may have in my suitcase. Of course, I came with plenty of the New York uniform, meaning lots of black. Apryl scoffs at the cowardly idea. Her wardrobe is an accurate reflection of the world she's created around her—lots of bold color and pattern statements everywhere.*

Dylan's bedroom. Apryl always told her that wherever she goes, there's a ray of sunshine above her. So they took it one step further by applying some masking tape and paint and made a big ray of yellow sunshine on the ceiling. Apryl believes it's easy to make something personal while keeping it simple.

When you make different choices, choices that people aren't used to or haven't seen before—like the ones Apryl has made in her condominium—you often face resistance from those that work with you. She faced many challenges achieving the look she wanted and admits getting there didn't win her any popularity contests. She has the strength of character and self-confidence to carry off her ideas, but finds that the construction world is still a man's world. She was blessed with many talented subcontractors who helped her through the process by pushing their own boundaries to find the look she wanted. As an example, the Venetian plaster contains layers of

< (opposite, top) APRYL'S BEDROOM IS OFTEN THE EARLY-MORNING MEETING PLACE FOR HER AND THE GIRLS. THE CORK WALLPAPER WAS A LITTLE TOO MONOTONOUS FOR APRYL, SO SHE CUT OUT SHAPES AND ADDED COLORFUL ACETATE INSERTS.

∨ (bottom right and left) tHE MASTER BATH IS A SPONTANEOUS WORK OF ART. WHEN THE PLASTER-WORK BEGAN, APRYL SCRAMBLED TO FIND COINS AND OTHER OBJECTS, INCLUDING HER FINGERS, TO CREATE SWIRLS OF DESIGNS. THE CABINETS DISPLAY VARIOUS KNOBS AND PULLS, AND THE TILEWORK CONTAINS EVERYTHING FROM GLASS TO PLASTIC BEADS.

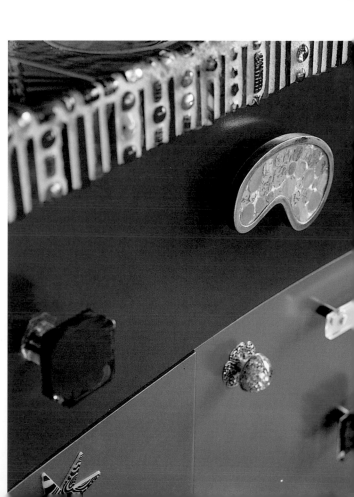

> THE KITCHEN CABINETS ARE PAINTED A METALLIC BLUE WITH CUT-OUT SHAPES OF DIFFERENT COLORS ADDED FOR INTEREST.

∧ APRYL'S JEWELRY DESIGN IS WHAT INSPIRED HER TO FILL THE PLEXIGLAS LEG OF THEIR KITCHEN TABLE. THE CONTENTS INCLUDE ALL KINDS OF BEADS AND PLASTIC OBJECTS THAT CAUGHT HER EYE. SHE COMMENTS, "IT TOOK A LONG TIME."

purple, green, and red—colors that are relatively new to this ancient craft—but Apryl encouraged the use of a more exciting palette. Using materials in offbeat applications is also one of her trademarks. The jewelry designer in Apryl couldn't resist applying beads in her mosaic tile designs in the bathrooms. Her cork wallpaper in the bedroom has cut-out shapes where color patches are inset to add interest. The "thinking outside the box" style is what makes Apryl's home for her and her girls such a delight to the senses.

Apryl's hope for the environment she's created is that her friends and family who enter her home "feel an exuberance, a sense of the possibilities that life has to offer. Perhaps the best is yet to come. We can go forward only by looking both outside and within ourselves. Yet the farthest, longest, deepest journey we must make is the one within. I want people to feel connected simultaneously to the exterior surroundings and to the deeper meaning within—to be touched by my struggle, but to know that there is a positive to the emerging because life is a series of conflicts and blossoming." It's a tall order for any dwelling, but Apryl has succeeded in creating a home that stimulates and inspires while offering comfort and refuge. There is much to explore within the confines of Apryl's walls, and her creative spirit inspires any visitor to play in his or her own world.

➥ *Apryl and I brain-storm about how we'll make our picture together. Before long we're putting on bangles, necklaces, hats, and earrings. Somehow this magical coloring-book home in the clouds invites playtime, so playing dress-up for the photo comes naturally. Laughing, I feel like a 6-year-old, and we smile for the camera. I realize that what happens here in this fairy-tale setting has to do with letting go and finding that childlike spirit within. Apryl's work was finding her own child spirit and saying, "Yes!" She lets that child rule when it comes to all her design choices. That is where the magic begins.*

HEAVENLY HAVEN

∧ CLARE CALDER-MARSHALL ON THE LEFT AND ALISON ENGLEFIELD ON THE RIGHT.

< (left, opposite) THE WHITE-WASHED INTERIOR AND THE ADDITION OF RICH JEWEL TONES MAKE THE CHAPEL A WARM LIVING ENVIRONMENT. A UNIQUE PENDANT LIGHT IS MADE FROM FOUND BEACH TREASURES.

→ I ventured to the Lands End Peninsula in Cornwall because it contains England's second-largest population of artists next to London. Finding artists here is one of the easiest tasks I've faced. The western-most village of St. Just sits atop rugged moorland and looks toward the spectacular coast of the Atlantic. The awesome views and bucolic landscape of this area are a natural magnet for artists. Buildings that seem to have grown from the rocky earth form the stony architecture of the town. It is in the heart of St. Just where I find the old stone chapel that is the home and studio of artists Alison Englefield and Clare Calder-Marshall.

The Old Sunday School studio and gallery is a cornerstone of the history of the village of St. Just. The chapel and adjoining cottage were built in 1755 and are ripe with centuries of stories and interesting tenants. The history, however, is debatably no match for the current incarnation as the home and work space of painter and textile artist Alison Englefield and film and video artist Clare Calder-Marshall. Alison and Clare weren't shopping for a church for their next home, but when they were offered the opportunity to buy this little piece of heaven, they jumped at the chance. A popular vacation destination and one that Alison had visited as a child, the village of St. Just was the ideal location—close to the ocean, surrounded by rolling heaths, and thick with artists. More than 50 artists live and work in this tiny town. It's only fitting that a dream led Alison to this other-worldly home.

Since 1998, Alison and Clare have called the sanctuary home. The old stone walls house the gallery at the front of the church where Alison's work of poured-pulp landscapes and angelic portraits are on display, as well as a whimsical line of jewelry and her now-famous collection of paintings of the windswept "Ladies of St. Just."
Entering into the sanctuary, which is the living room, is breathtaking. Volumes of space above, without the pews below, translate into lots of room to create. Alison and Clare redesigned the second-floor balcony that wraps around the interior and provides the space for Alison's art studio and their bedroom. Alison admits, "Living in a chapel is inspiring and expansive."

Alison and Clare's chapel embodies all that is sacred in a home. The architecture sets the tone, and their feminine touches have further enhanced the graceful dwelling by draping soft, sheer curtains in jewel tones. The sacred space had been used as residence before Alison and Clare's purchase, but they renovated the loft and made

^ THE LOFT AREA, LOOKING
TOWARD THE BEDROOM
ON ONE END AND THE
STUDIO ON THE OTHER.
THE LARGE SCULPTURES
WERE USED IN A THEATER
PRODUCTION.

> THE ENTRANCE TO THE
OLD SUNDAY-SCHOOL
GALLERY.

I'm beginning to learn about this area, which is steeped in mysticism. Religious icons, graveyards, frescoes, and stone circles are all part of the heritage. The countryside evokes a sense of awe as well as reverence. The dramatic coast, the winding, narrow lanes, and the rolling, green hills framed by thick stone walls are all part of the charm and allure that captures anyone who visits. There is nothing more fitting to my exploration into the rich lore of Cornwall than the village chapel and its inspired occupants.

> THE VIEW FROM THE DINING ROOM IS FRAMED IN COLORS OF RED AND BLUE IN THE KITCHEN.

> (opposite) ALISON DEMONSTRATES HER METHOD OF POURED-PULP PAINTING, USING A HANDMADE PAPER.

many small improvements to make their house their own. The adjoining cottage, formerly the meetinghouse, was transformed into a small vacation rental. A garden connects the areas in the back and is often the chosen spot for afternoon tea.

As with most of the townspeople, walks to the sea are a part of daily life for Alison and Clare. The artists' community that is so predominant in Cornwall is here largely because of the stunning beauty of the coastal landscapes. Alison draws many of her creative ideas from her walks along the beach. Undoubtedly, life along the coast is always an inspiration, but Alison says, "Living in a sacred place has brought sacred symbols to the fore in my work." Her poured-pulp paintings often appear as a shrouded face and have an ethereal quality, seeming to peer from the paper as if in a fresco. The spiritual environment also influences Clare's video work, such as her latest documentary called "Sanctuary," based on a ruined 18th-century church.

Alison and Clare truly represent artists whose work is inseparable from where they live. The chapel has become not only the environment in which they live and work but also the place where they draw much of their inspiration and ideas for their art. Whether it's used as a theater, for entertaining, or for producing or showing their work, the Old Sunday School is truly their haven, the place they call home, and the place from where their work emerges.

➠ *As I leave the Old Sunday School and say goodbye to my new friends, the wind has picked up, and the gray skies have turned to rain. It only adds to the dramatic atmosphere of St. Just and the powerfully creative lives I've encountered inside the church. I'm reflecting on the nurturing quality that living in a former place of worship must have on Alison and Clare. To be able to draw upon that resource has had an immense influence on the direction of their lives. And just as I'm packing up the last of my things the wind blows some notes away. I imagine myself as one of the characters in Alison's painting,* Ladies of St. Just, *getting tossed about in the strong Cornwall spring winds to my next artist's sanctuary.*

ODE TO SOUTHERN ROOTS

< WILLIE LITTLE IN HIS FAVORITE, BIG ROCKING CHAIR.

> (below, opposite) SELF-PORTRAIT OF WILLIE AS A CHILD. THE FIREPLACE MANTLE IS ARTFULLY ARRANGED WITH WILLIE'S COLLECTIONS. ON CLOSER INSPECTION, THE STILL LIFE REVEALS RUSTED CANS AND FLEA-MARKET FINDS.

→◆ *Two of the finest galleries in Charlotte, North Carolina, have recommended that I visit artist Willie Little. I make my way to his urban neighborhood, and perhaps it is no coincidence that what I find is, well, little. The unassuming exterior belies the world that waits inside. Willie welcomes me into his home, apologizing for the disarray because he has just finished an extended residency at the Marin Headlands Center for the Arts in California. He loved his work there and the exciting world of San Francisco, but the South is his home and getting back to this place is getting back to his roots and the subjects that inspire him.*

The small bungalow that was built in the '20s is the ideal container for artist Willie Little. Like so many artists, he loves flea-market finds and all kinds of collectibles, but unlike others, he brings a statement of his cultural traditions and his strong Southern heritage to all that he collects for his home and for his fine-art pieces.

Willie was born and raised in the rural town of Little Washington, North Carolina, and carries the memories of his childhood and those simpler days into the work that has made him one of the most successful emerging artists of the South. His home and his work evoke a feeling of his past. From portraits of him as a child to tools his grandmother used for gardening, they are all a part of the many

< TWO DIFFERENT CORNERS OF THE HOUSE ARE STILL-LIFE ASSEMBLAGES. EACH WALL DISPLAYS A PIECE FROM HIS SERIES, "THROUGH THE WINDOW INTO MY GRANDMOTHER'S GARDEN." THE RUSTIC CHAIRS, TABLES, AND FLEA-MARKET FINDS COMPLETE THE SCENE.

vignettes that Willie constructs at home. Each room is full of thoughtful still lifes, some with a corner that contains found objects along with one of Willie's assemblages. Willie strives to bring the country he loves into his city home. The effect is one of balancing elegant composition with rustic style. Willie knows it's important to be true to yourself when it comes to your surroundings. He believes that filling your space with the objects that ground you is critical to well-being. "Find things that speak to you so when you put them together they tell a story."

Willie graduated from the University of North Carolina with a bachelor's degree and began his career focusing on two- and three-dimensional works. From his installation piece, *Juke Joint*, which features an interactive multimedia work about his father's illegal liquor house, to his body of work "Through the Window into My Grandmother's Garden," to the series "Black As...," which looks beyond the stereotype and conventional ideas regarding skin color within the African American community, Willie's art is all about the

➥ *Willie is a bit shy at first, but after we've listened to a few good India.Arie songs on his stereo, the conversation immediately shifts to his passion for art and the art of living. The attention to detail in his surroundings is evidence of his sensitivity and appreciation for beauty. Every artist has a unique definition of beauty. Discovering the aesthetics of Willie means exploring his family, his past, and the cultural traditions that have shaped him into who he is today.*

place he comes from. He retells and reclaims the stories, rural colloquialisms, and family history through his art. Although Willie celebrates his rural upbringing, the city is where he thrives. Willie says, "My art is an expression of who I am. My home is an expression of my art. To enter into one is to enter into both. It is my hope that when friends enter my home, they immediately begin to understand more of who I am."

Willie is warm and engaging. His home is a mirror of the person who embraces the simple country roots with his intriguing compositions and comfortable corners. He says, "My home, like my art, is engaging, exciting, revealing, and seductive. The work seduces the visitors' thoughts about what it is to be an artist and a Southerner and ultimately allows visitors to think about the universal nature of life and experiences we all share. When I entertain, people want to explore the nooks and crannies, and I welcome that."

^ WILLIE NEVER MISSES AN OPPORTUNITY TO CREATE A COZY VIGNETTE IN HIS ENVI-
RONMENT. HIS COUCH IS SURROUNDED BY HIS CLEVER DISPLAYS.

< (opposite) THIS ARRANGEMENT'S FOCAL POINT IS FROM HIS POIGNANT SERIES,
"BLACK AS..."

●● *I'm curious about the world in which Willie grew up and the hardships of the rural South in the '60s, but the Willie of today is a success story. As a result of studying around the country and receiving various grants and fellowships, he has come a long distance from the one-room house in eastern North Carolina.*

The big rocker in Willie's house is an ironic touch of decorating. His light-hearted prodding invites you to ask about the over-sized object in the "Little" house. He laughs at the interest in it and says he would question anyone who wouldn't inquire about the oversized seat in his small living room. Scale and size aside, Willie just liked the humor of it. "Little" comes up for Willie a lot. From the town he grew up in, Little Washington, to his name, the metaphors are hard to resist. I haven't met any-one quite like him. With all he has accomplished and his infectious enthusiasm, I can't help but say that "Big" is really what Willie Little is all about.

LUNA PARC

^ PORTRAIT OF THE KING OF LUNA PARC, RICKY BOSCARINO.

^ (top right) THE FRONT OF RICKY'S HOUSE IS AN EVER-CHANGING SCENE HE CHARTS IN PHOTOGRAPHS. THE WALL AND THE SCULPTURE ON TOP OF THE HOUSE ARE RECENT ADDITIONS.

> IT'S TWILIGHT, AND THE WOODS LIGHT UP. RICKY'S MOSAIC SCULPTURES AND OTHER ARTFUL ARRANGEMENTS LINE THE PATHS TO THE STUDIO.

> (far right) THE OUTSIDE WALLS ARE JUST ANOTHER CANVAS COVERED IN TILE, BEER CAPS, COPPER SHEETING, AND ANYTHING ELSE THAT INSPIRES RICKY.

➽ *My interest in Luna Parc began long before I made my way through the woods to Ricky Boscarino's wondrous world. Although I'd been on his virtual tour, nothing can compare to the unreal reality that he has created. Imagine* Alice in Wonderland *meets the Technicolor Munchkin Land in the* Wizard of Oz. *The entry gate with the auspicious Tibetan greeting* Om Mani Padme Hum *blesses all who venture through the clever version of a beaded curtain of hanging chains and pool balls. Following the tiled yellow-brick road—some of Ricky's first mosaic work on the property—I'm already dazed and overwhelmed—a feeling I'll have for my entire visit to this colorful land of lunacy.*

Ricky Boscarino's home is sculpture in the form of a residence and playground. Although the design and creation of Luna Parc is one of the many forms of art that Ricky has perfected, the home and all that surrounds it are a monument to his bottomless well of innovation. Colors, materials, sculptures, lighting, and design are used in ways far beyond the conventional. There is nothing ordinary about this fairy-tale world. This tiny, rough, hunting cabin in the isolated countryside at the edge of the Poconos in New Jersey has seen an evolution that began 14 years ago and continues to evolve today.

There is no logical place to begin to describe Luna Parc. Shortly after he purchased the house, Ricky started his renovations to turn the summer camp into a year-round residence, including windows, new electric service, and insulation, doing most of the work

There are endless potential photos at Luna Parc. I don't know how to edit myself and all the possibilities for a visual story. Ricky works away on his new 500-square-foot (46.5-square-meter) studio for his kiln and ceramics—not surprising, it will be covered with mosaic tile—while I explore. I am amazed by the amount of labor and commitment that Ricky has invested in this place. Every turn reveals a detail or a quirky element I haven't seen before. From his fascinating collections to the surprising use of materials and objects in completely unique ways, I am overwhelmed by his creative energy. As the day progresses I've "caught" this bug that seems to emanate from Luna Parc, one of continued inspiration as I obsessively photograph and keep riding the creative wave until well after the sun sets.

himself. At the same time he was doing about 30 shows a year selling his line of custom jewelry designs. Ricky had no particular plan in mind. He says, "My master plan was to have no master plan. I want things to evolve and overlap. I try not to take things apart; I just keep adding to them."

The bathroom was the first major addition to the house, taking five years to complete and using more than 984,000 tiles on the inside alone. Ricky stopped counting tiles after he completed the inside. All the exterior walls of the bathroom are also covered in mosaics. The inspiration for the bathroom came from two different trips to Europe, one to visit the Roman baths in Italy and the other to visit

the Turkish baths in Budapest. The addition of the bathroom was a sensual statement and significantly increased the square footage of the house. His most recent addition is the 100-foot (30.5-meter) wall at the front of the cottage. The Gaudi-like structure frames the house with pinnacles and rounded shapes. The formidable task of tiling the entire surface is still in progress. Winding your way toward the studio is another journey into mosaicland. Tiled sculptures of various sizes that light up like Christmas trees are scattered along the wooded path. An occasional shopping cart filled with odd glass balls or color-coordinated bottles are parked along the way. A turn in the path leads to the little sanctuary, an inspiring addition to the compound. A purple building with chartreuse trim, the chapel is covered with crutches. The tongue-in-cheek testament to being saved is, at the same time, a serious meditation retreat for Ricky. The stained-glass windows that Ricky made fill the tiny room with heavenly colors in the early morning light.

< (opposite) THE LAVENDER CHAPEL OF THE SAINTS WAS INSPIRED BY RICKY'S GRANDFATHER, WHO WITNESSED A MIRACLE IN SICILY OF A CRIPPLED BOY WHO WAS HEALED AND RAN TO HIS MOTHER. HE WOULD WEEP AS HE TOLD THE STORY TO RICKY, SAYING HE WOULD NEVER FORGET.

∧ (above) THE LIVING ROOM IS FRAMED BY THE LARGE, CIRCULAR WINDOW, WHICH LOOKS OUT ON THE FRONT GARDENS. RICKY'S CHEERFUL PAINT COLORS SERVE AS A BACKDROP FOR HIS ENDLESS COLLECTIONS, INCLUDING RELIGIOUS ICONS, MUSICAL INSTRUMENTS, AND HAND-BLOWN GLASS, TO NAME A FEW.

→ I realize as I'm finishing my second day of photographing at Luna Parc that the next time I visit, the images I've made will be dated— this world, this live-in sculpture, is continually changing, constantly evolving. There is pride and ownership here that goes beyond the average person's commitment to a place. Ricky often refers to Luna Parc as his kingdom and rightly so. No king puts more work into his land and home than Ricky. To commemorate his reign, he constructed a beautiful crown with an amethyst that rests on top of the purple velvet and gold. It's only fitting that we have a photo of the king atop the house, surveying the kingdom below. Ricky transports me to the land of kings and kingdoms and fantasylands for a bit longer before I have to travel beyond this fairy tale to more adventures and stories down the road.

The exterior, the grounds, and all the outbuildings have a presence of their own, but the interior of the house is truly a museum. Filled with collections of everything from colanders hanging in the kitchen to bottle-cap–covered walls, the home is a statement of eclectic and ingenious style. Colorful stars, stripes, and checks are all part of the backdrop for Ricky's passionate collecting. The living room is full of musical instruments, comfy pillows, angel lamps, and hundreds of Buddha statues. The kitchen is a creative domain for Ricky that goes beyond cooking. The sink is an old tin washtub resting on bowling balls. Ladles and pots of all shapes and sizes hang from above.

It's only natural that a museum like Luna Parc has a constant stream of visitors. Ricky opens his doors a couple times a year for tours to the public and regularly brings school children through. He always has an open door for kids, because he believes it's important to teach children how to live and accept things that are "outside the box." Ricky's own upbringing was supportive and nontraditional. He was the only child of three to attend art school (he graduated from Rhode Island School of Design), but all went on to pursue careers in art.

When asked about the secret to the continual flow of art and sculpting of this woodland wonderland, Ricky explains, "The most important aspect of my work at Luna Parc is that I'm committed to spending the rest of my life at this house. That has freed up any idea of resale value or 20th-century concepts of why you shouldn't paint with wild colors or put your personal stamp on your home. Make a commitment to the home and forget about resale value." Ricky says, "With all the beautiful colors in the world, why would you settle for white?"

< THE DINING ROOM IS OFTEN
FULL OF GUESTS. RICKY
LOVES TO COOK AND ENTER-
TAIN, AND IN A SETTING LIKE
THIS, THE PARTY IS SURE TO
BE LIVELY. UNLIKELY ITEMS
HANG FROM THE HIGH CEIL-
INGS, SUCH AS CHAIRS,
INSTRUMENTS, AND GLOBES,
WITH PLANT VINES WRAPPING
AROUND IT ALL.

∨ THE KITCHEN IS SMALL BUT
EFFICIENT. CORKS PAPER THE
WALLS, AND MULTICOLORED
COLANDERS HANG FROM
ABOVE. THE OLD TIN WASH-
TUBS WITH CONTEMPORARY
PLUMBING REST CAREFULLY
ON BOWLING BALLS.

LOFTY BOSTON

^ JOANNE KALIONTZIS, COLLAGE ARTIST AND GRAPHIC
  DESIGNER, SITTING IN FRONT OF ONE HER LARGE
  COLLAGES. SHE'S ONE OF THE MOVERS AND SHAKERS
  WHO KEEPS FORT POINT RUNNING AND IS ACTIVE IN
  THE MOVEMENT TO SAVE THE STUDIOS.

> JOANNE'S LIGHT-FILLED, ANGULAR FLOOR PLAN IN HER
  STUDIO ON SUMMER STREET.

∧ (top, left) GABRIELLE SCHAFFNER, HER PARTNER LAURA DAVIDSON, AND THEIR DAUGHTER WERE AMONG THE FIRST TO START THE COOPERATIVE MOVEMENT IN THE FORT POINT AREA. GABRIELLE IS A CERAMIC ARTIST. LAURA'S MEDIUMS INCLUDE PAINTING, MIXED MEDIA, AND ART BOOKS.

∧ (top, right) VIEWS OF DOWNTOWN BOSTON AND THE HARBOR FROM THE SUMMER STREET ROOFTOP GARDEN.

∧ (bottom) THE SPACE THAT GABRIELLE AND HER FAMILY HAVE CREATED.

The transformation of the Fort Point area began in earnest in the early '90s. Groups of artists joined forces and, after a tremendous amount of dedication and hundreds of volunteer hours, created the cooperatives that purchased these "undesirable" warehouses that would become home. In the case of 300 Summer Street Studios, there are 48 artist-owners. With little money down and some financial finagling, the old building gained a new life. The owners—who are required to be artists—created individual lofts that are a loft-dweller's dream. Minimally finished when the building was renovated for living spaces, each owner designed and built one-of a-kind

∧ ARTIST ROB REEPS AND HIS WIFE KAREN CLEBER IN HIS PAINTING STUDIO.

> (opposite, top) KAREN AND ROB'S LOFT AT SUMMER STREET SHOWCASES HIS LARGE OIL PAINTINGS. THEY ADDED NEW FLOORS, KITCHEN UPGRADES, AND DIVIDING WALLS FOR PRIVACY IN THEIR SPACE.

> (opposite, bottom left) MARIE GALVIN SHOWS OFF HER ARTISTIC HEADGEAR. HER WORK FEATURES A NEW TWIST ON MILLINERY.

> (opposite, bottom right) MARIE'S LOFT HAS A COMMON AREA SHE AND HER HUSBAND SHARE WITH THREE OTHER STUDIOS. ALTHOUGH THEY HAVE A LOOSE COOPERATIVE WITH THE OTHER ARTISTS, THEY DON'T OWN THEIR SPACES ON MELCHER STREET. TALK OF A CORPORATE PURCHASE WOULD MEAN THEY'D BE FORCED TO LEAVE.

Each loft I visited has a truly unique style that is as varied as the people who inhabit them. Although they started with similar shells, these talented artists have created dwellings that are one-of-a-kind environments. Walking from loft to loft, being greeted by a warm welcome behind every door, and seeing the incredible art that spills into the halls of these large buildings is exhilarating.

spaces to fit his or her unique requirements and tastes. Large windows that frame the harbor views, high ceilings, and old wooden floors are all part of the package. Some owners, as in the case of architect and photographer Jeffrey Heyne and his wife Dorothea Van Camp, a painter and mixed-media artist, have made strong architectural statements. Others have dressed and transformed the generous square footage in a less formal manner, such as pinhole photographer Jesseca Ferguson and husband Mark Pevsner, a pianist and composer.

Developing the building to accommodate the various artists and their multitude of uses required a great deal of planning. An advisory board was formed that continues to keep the cooperative running smoothly. Among the many things living at the Summer Street complex offers are freight elevators, a cooperative gallery that showcases artists of Fort Point, a common area rooftop garden, a frame shop, and one of the neighborhood's best lunch spots.

∧ PINHOLE PHOTOGRAPHER JESSECA FERGUSON IN HER ENVIABLE STUDIO. HER HUSBAND MARK PEVSNER IS A COMPOSER AND MUSICIAN HARD AT WORK AT THE OTHER END OF THEIR LOFT.

> JESSECA AND MARK HAVE A FUNKY, COMFORTABLE STYLE AT THEIR SUMMER STREET LOFT.

> PAINTER DOROTHEA VAN CAMP AND HER HUSBAND,
ARCHITECT AND PHOTOGRAPHIC ARTIST JEFFREY HEYNE.

∨ JEFFREY PUT HIS ARCHITECTURAL DESIGN SKILLS TO
WORK TO COME UP WITH A COLORFUL, CONTEMPORARY
LAYOUT IN THEIR LOFT. FROM GALVANIZED METAL TO
ORIENTED STRAND BOARD (OSB), MATERIALS WERE USED
IN UNIQUE AND UNCONVENTIONAL WAYS.

Around the corner on A Street is another thriving co-op with similar amenities. Gabrielle Schaffner and her partner Laura Davidson were two of the first artists to sign on with the idea of artists living cooperatively. They continue to contribute to the organization of the neighborhood and the yearly open-studio tours. Although only two buildings in the Fort Point area are cooperatively owned by artists, hundreds of artists in the neighborhood have shared living and communal spaces, such as the space where Marie Galvin, hat designer and headgear artist extraordinaire, lives and works. With every turn of the corner in this industrial borough, you'll find an innovative twist to living in the city.

As with most places that artists "discover," the Fort Point Channel area is facing the pressure of development. With the neighborhood having been transformed into a desirable area, the real estate prices are climbing, and big corporate entities want a slice of the pie. Some of the artists who haven't had the opportunity to buy into a cooperative are facing the probability of moving. It's a dilemma that is familiar to growth anywhere. Luckily, the Fort Point Cultural Coalition, which was formed to save the studios, is a strong group. Its mission is to preserve, promote, and expand the cultural community. Given the creative resources and the individuals who have brought this neighborhood to its present-day level of renown and success, Fort Point will continue to be a model for other cities to follow and a prospering haven for Boston artists for many years to come.

➼ *After a couple days of wonderful art and hard photography work, it's time to hit the local pub as well as get in a few last visits before I head out. I've made a dozen new friends in Boston whom I'm hoping I'll visit again soon. I can't wait to experiment with some ideas with my own photography, inspired by all the fascinating tools and techniques I've seen among the artists here. I imagine that to wake up breathing the art, surrounded by other successful artists in many different mediums, is reason enough to choose this vibrant community. To say that the environment here is stimulating is an understatement. This is the kind of feeling that could make me want to live part-time in my little mountain town and part-time in one of these fine Boston cooperatives, immersed in this creative realm with plenty of friends around at the end of the day.*

CORNISH COAST GUARD COTTAGE

< PETER EVELEIGH AND RACHEL CROSSLEY IN THEIR LIVING ROOM.

v RACHEL LANDSCAPED AND TRANSFORMED THE GARDENS THAT LOOK TO THE HEATHLANDS INTO A LUSH ENVIRONMENT.

> (opposite) THE DINING ROOM OFFERS A SOOTHING PALETTE OF COLORS. PETER'S PAINTINGS ARE DIS-PLAYED ON THE WALLS THROUGHOUT THE HOUSE.

Peter Eveleigh and Rachel Crossley needed to escape from their busy life near Bristol. Coming to Cornwall on frequent holidays, they found their bit of paradise. Finding property to buy in this popular seaside destination is difficult, but after months of searching, the opportunity arose to purchase the run-down Coast Guard cottage in the little village of Treen, and they acted quickly. They never dreamed the house would be so close to their favorite beach escape or have views that embrace the moorland. Peter and Rachel both got their degrees in art. Peter pursued his painting career and taught for many years at Henbury School in Bristol. That's where he first met Rachel, who was a student. Years later they bumped into each other at one of his exhibitions, and before long they were planning their move to the country.

∧ PETER AND RACHEL'S KITCHEN WAS A BIG PART OF THEIR REMODEL EXPENSE. THE KITCHEN'S SOFT BLUE-GREEN COMPLEMENTS THE VIEW OUT THE WINDOW TO THE GARDENS AND THE HEATHLAND BEYOND.

Peter's abstract painting is rich with the themes of nature, gardens, and their beloved beach, which is a stone's throw away from the cottage. His bright, abstract paintings taken from his sketches are a vivid interpretation of his surroundings. The magical light, the rocky cliffs, and their abundant garden are the inspiration for his art. Peter says, "It's taken me 40 years to find my language, and it could only have happened here." Walks along the shore and a brisk dip in the ocean are part of the daily routine for Peter and Rachel. Among many of her talents, she is a ceramic artist, jewelry designer, and furniture designer. Her eye for transforming the old cottage came from her natural talent and her professional training. On the outside, she has transformed their yard into an English garden worthy of envy. Other locals have recognized her gift and have hired her to work her magic in their gardens, including those of a local hotel. Peter and Rachel's combined visual experience have helped them to create a home of simple, harmonious design.

Rachel finds the secret to her success with decorating is starting with a fabric she likes and choosing complementary colors and accessories. The limited access to a variety of home furnishings in this rural area means frequent trips to the city for lighting, hardware, and furniture purchases.

To update the 1926 house, they rewired the electrical system and installed new plumbing throughout, demolished many walls, installed central heating, and established the garden. They also completely gutted and remodeled the kitchen. The renovation took 18 months to complete. Sunny days were spent lounging on the beach, whereas the rainy days were spent working on the house.

➺ The quiet, misty day at the Coast Guard cottage is relaxing and comfortable. Peter and Rachel give me lots of "proper cups of tea" to keep me going. The peaceful atmosphere that prevails both inside the house and outside is intoxicating. Peter and Rachel are working in their studios, and it's clear the nurturing quality of their home gently supports their creativity. I'm immediately at ease here and know that that is most likely one of the feelings they wanted to evoke in their home.

< DETAIL OF THE GLASS DISPLAY
BETWEEN THE LIVING ROOM
AND KITCHEN.

> (opposite, top) THE GOLDEN
LIVING ROOM WITH THE CHEER-
FUL FIREPLACE PAINTED IN
CHARTREUSE BRIGHTENS ANY
FOGGY DAY ON THE COAST. THE
FIREPLACE BECOMES AN ALTAR
OF SORTS, WITH SPRING FLOW-
ERS, A CANDLE, AND ONE OF
RACHEL'S SCULPTURES.

> (opposite, bottom) PETER AT
WORK IN HIS LIGHT-FILLED
STUDIO SURROUNDED BY HIS
GOUACHE PAINTINGS.

Rachel says, "I wanted the color inside me to come out in the home." Careful thought was given to the colors that are seen from one room to the next, as well as the colors that are reflected in the landscape outside the windows. The muted tones of the moorlands that surround the house are a rich palette to emulate.

Peter and Rachel both want their home to be a place of inspiration, just as the surrounding village and landscape are an inspiration to them. Peter says, "I hope that visitors are visually, mentally, and emotionally stimulated. I want people to be excited and have good, strong, positive feelings being here." They have managed to turn their vacation destination into their dream home, one that nurtures their artistic endeavors and is close to their cherished seaside activities—a home that embraces the history of the area while providing a contemporary coastal retreat.

CAROLINA CONTEMPORARY

< ERIC ANDERSON IN HIS JAPANESE-INSPIRED
GARDEN.

> (opposite) ERIC'S PAINTINGS AND THE
DINING ROOM CHAIRS WORK TOGETHER
FOR A HARMONIOUS STILL LIFE.

^ (above) THE LIVING ROOM IS BALANCED SYMMETRY
WITH ERIC'S PIECES ON DISPLAY. A LARGE WALL OF
WINDOWS PROVIDES A FLOW FROM INSIDE TO THE
PRIVATE GARDEN.

> (opposite) THE DINING AREA ADJOINS THE LIVING
ROOM. ERIC'S LARGE MIXED-MEDIA CONSTRUCTION
BECKONS FOR A CLOSER LOOK. PAINTING THAT
APPEARS TO BE METAL AND DELICATELY CRAFTED
WOODWORK ARE PART OF THIS CONSTRUCTION.

Eric Anderson and his wife, Jennifer, have designed a home that functions as a gallery-like backdrop and is meant to be a showplace for his work, as well as their escape from the chaotic world. The result is a contemplative, comfortable environment with Eric's colorful mixed-media constructions thoughtfully displayed. Eric believes, "To relegate objects of art to a place where they don't have significance or don't have a domain where they can really function is disrespectful. It's like going to a concert and talking over the musicians' playing." Eric believes in culling some of his best pieces from a series he's working on and living with those pieces on his walls. Prominently displaying his work at home is crucial to his development. The process of learning from his own art continues as he observes and gathers important information for his next work. Serving as reminders, his art and that of other artists he admires give him pleasure and drive him to create more.

➡ This rainy autumn day has set the stage for a contemplative mood in Charlotte, North Carolina. The cool, austere home of artist and longtime professor Eric Anderson is my destination and the ideal complement to the day. The flat-roofed, contemporary home is nestled into the wooded neighborhood. Japanese-style gardens invite and draw me into the house. The feeling upon entering is that this home and Eric's art are synchronized. His art works beautifully in this setting, and the architectural influence is evident in his work.

Eric and his wife bought this house about 14 years ago. It was a unique '50s modern home in a traditional neighborhood. Eric liked the way it blended into the environment. They did some major renovations, including knocking out walls and adding new floors. Eric believes that art and architecture need to reflect the art and materials of the present day, so finding a house that fit current styles and trends was an important factor.

Eric's work employs contemporary materials and colors with modern construction and engineering. He uses rubber, metal, and wood, which, when combined, seem to transcend the materials. Eric graduated with a master's degree in fine arts from Pratt and went on to teach at the University of North Carolina, where he's been since 1967. His work is collected and shown around the country. His wife, Jennifer, is a practicing therapist, so they have designed their home to accommodate her office as well. Eric's studio is a short walk away in the neighborhood.

Eric believes that creating your own sanctuary is about getting in touch with your creativity. For him, the environment is a physical extension of a person's expression. At the end of every semester, Eric brings his students from his senior seminar over to his home. He says, "They are always delighted and surprised and comment that they never really knew how artists live." Eric says, "If my students at least learn how to live with an awareness aesthetically, I would be totally satisfied." Given Eric's depth and ability to communicate ideas and philosophy, rest assured there are many gifted artists that have been inspired by his teachings and the way he lives.

^ THE GALLERY-LIKE SITTING AREA WITH THE BREUER CHAIRS, ERIC'S MIXED-MEDIA PAINTING CONSTRUCTION, AND SCULPTURES OFFERS A CONTEMPORARY ENVIRONMENT.

< THE COZY CORNER OF THE DEN IS FRAMED BY ONE OF ERIC'S MIXED-MEDIA WORKS.

GOING DUTCH

< YVONNE'S CLASSIC DINING ROOM OCCUPIES ONE
OF THE WINGS OF HER HOME. HER SMALL BRONZE
SCULPTURES GRACE THE MANTEL.

^ (center) YVONNE'S LIVING ROOM IS A MIX OF CLAS-
SIC ARCHITECTURE WITH CONTEMPORARY ACCENTS.
THE SPARSE DECOR SHOWS OFF HER BRONZE
SCULPTURES.

^ (right) YVONNE PILLER AND MARGA WURPEL AT
YVONNE'S BACK DOOR.

A short train ride out of bustling Amsterdam in a quiet, suburban neighborhood lives two friends and artists, Marga Wurpel and Yvonne Piller. Their friendship and close physical proximity made their stories similar, yet their style and art defines their entirely individual expression. My trip to visit Marga and Yvonne is one filled with the finest Dutch hospitality. Marga's husband Richard goes out of his way to bring us lunch and my newfound favorite Dutch treat, french fries and kroketten. Moving between the houses during the day offers a broader and more complete view of this community and the artists I'm photographing.

∧ THE CLASSIC ARCHITECTURE OF YVONNE'S HOME IS PRESERVED AS A HISTORICAL HOME WITH PROTECTIVE COVENANTS.

> YVONNE'S GARDEN SERVES AS A PERFECT GALLERY FOR HER BRONZE HORSES. THIS SCULPTURE IS FRAMED BY HER FRONT ENTRY.

Yvonne Piller's work of cast bronze consists mainly of horses and the human figure, and the statues grace all corners of the home and garden. She uses the magnificent backdrop of her early 20th-century home to showcase her art. Frequently she removes her personal effects and turns the house and garden into a gallery of fine bronze sculptures.

Seventeen years ago, she and her husband bought this unique and historical property in Santpoort, Netherlands. Yvonne had always admired this house, and it was a stroke of good luck and timing that they were able to purchase it. The house, built in 1911, is a famous example of Jugendstil and Art Deco design. It is a designated historical structure and must remain true to its original design. The only renovations that have taken place are the remodeling of the kitchen and bathrooms. The exterior must remain unchanged. The floor plan, Yvonne says, is a butterfly style with the wings stretching from the center. The cool color palette complements the frequently overcast skies in Holland. The living and dining rooms each occupy a separate wing, creating defined and cozy spaces.

Yvonne's bronzes are perhaps best viewed in her stately garden. The garden and yard is a rare and much cherished luxury in a country so short of land. Yvonne takes full advantage of the grounds to display her figures. Yvonne says, "Because I exhibit my work at my house and sell my sculptures myself, I do my utmost to make people feel welcome and encourage them to look around."

➥ Yvonne, Marga, and I spend a pleasant morning and lunch together. It's easy to see how they became good friends, sharing their mutual love of art, living nearby, and creating attractive home environments that can best show their work. We are brainstorming as to how best to tell their stories in the book when it occurs to me that showing their art and homes through their friendship makes for a different angle. So often our lives are influenced by the friends and people around us. Marga and Yvonne's lives intersect in rich ways that only those of friends can.

A short distance away, Marga Wurpel has a sculpture garden and home of her own, which speaks to her light-hearted nature. As you enter the house you are drawn to the sun-filled patio that leads to the garden. Wisteria drapes overhead, creating an inviting outdoor dining area and a perfect viewing spot for her sculptures. Marga works in clay, and she places her whimsical figures so they peek out of hidden corners in the garden.

Marga began her ceramics in 1975, studying in Amsterdam and Velsen. She participates in many exhibitions, and in a recent exhibition one piece was selected for Queen Beatrix in honor of her birthday. The ceramic crown was delicately crafted with a light-hearted feeling.

Inside, Marga and Richard created a cheery environment that features a mix of contemporary and antique furnishings in light-filled rooms. Their love of the Mediterranean has influenced their color and design choices throughout the house. The house has many large picture windows that frame the garden views, often including one of her humorous animal sculptures. Marga says, "My husband and I tried to create a vibrant atmosphere in both our home and garden that pleases and stimulates us." Marga and Richard take a great deal of pride in the environment they have created. Marga says, "When people visit my home I want them to feel warmly welcome and at ease and at the same time curious and stimulated by the living environment I have created inside and out."

> (opposite, top left) ON THE WURPELS' WISTERIA-COVERED PATIO, MARGA'S PICASSO-LIKE SCULPTURE SETS THE SCENE FOR AN AFTERNOON GLASS OF WINE.

> (opposite, top right) THE GRACEFUL ENTRY TO MARGA AND RICHARD'S HOME DISPLAYS A CELTIC HARP THAT LOOKS DIRECTLY TO THEIR GARDEN.

> (opposite, bottom) THEIR LIVING ROOM EMBRACES WARM MEDITERRANEAN COLORS AND IS FULL OF MARGA'S WHIMSICAL CLAY SCULPTURES.

➡ As we finish the day in Marga and Richard's garden, we enjoy a glass of wine before Richard rushes me to the train. Yvonne and Marga have introduced me to a side of Holland that I would have never seen as a tourist. By welcoming me into their homes and showing me the way they live with their art and the way their homes have a positive influence on their creative endeavors, I have a window on two talented artists and two good friends and neighbors in the Netherlands.

MASTER OF MUD

∧ PORTRAIT OF GERNOT IN HIS NATURALIZED GARDEN.

< THE DOMED WINDOWS PEEK THROUGH THE SOD ROOF OF GERNOT MINKE'S HOME, WHICH IS HARDLY DISTINGUISHABLE FROM THE SURROUNDING LANDSCAPE.

> LOOKING THROUGH THE DOORWAY INTO GERNOT'S LIBRARY THAT CIRCLES THE PERIMETER OF THE DOME.

> THE TUB IS BATHED IN LIGHT FROM THE SKYLIGHT, AND THE SURROUNDING MUD WALLS SHOW OFF GERNOT'S OIL PAINTINGS.

Located in a quiet suburb of Kassel, Germany, is the home of architect, artist, professor, and author Gernot Minke. His current home is the second he's designed and built in the neighborhood. Stepping inside the understated entry of his house, you realize that the space opens into a voluminous, light-filled dome rising 13 feet (4 meters) above. The clay bricks, which serve as building material throughout, circle around, layer upon layer, up to a circular glass skylight. From this central dome there are six other domed rooms, two framed with timbers, whereas the others are all constructed from clay. The floor plan resembles a honeycomb design and is a sculpture in every sense of the word. Gernot's years of studying and experimenting with earth construction produced a home that not only complements the environment but is also truly part of it.

Gernot, a professor at the University of Kassel and director of the Research Laboratory for Experimental Building, is a visionary and considered by many to be the European expert on clay and earth construction. His recently published book, now in English, *The Earth Construction Handbook*, is the bible of contemporary earth construction. Because he takes his inspiration from his travels around the world, the influence of a Moroccan mosque or a Navajo hogan is easy to extrapolate from Gernot's design. Although the style of construction for his home is more common in arid lands, Gernot has developed a formula that works for the damper climate of central Germany. The natural ability of clay to absorb and regulate humidity promotes a healthy environment and is ecologically beneficial. He has researched the properties of clay for 25 years and will readily list the benefits beyond its use as a building material.

^ GERNOT'S BATHROOM IS A FLUID SCULPTURE OF COILS OF CLAY. EVERY DETAIL WAS CREATED IN MUD PLASTER, FROM THE LEGS OF THE SINK TO THE ACTUAL BASIN—A COMPLETELY WATERPROOF AND PRACTICAL DESIGN.

ARTISTS' INTERIORS

➥ It's a lovely spring
day, and Gernot's garden
is bustling with birds and
the small pond outside is
teeming with life.
Walking around to catch
a view of the area, I realize I've walked up on the
roof of the house. The
plants in the surrounding
landscape blend with the
mix of grasses and flow-
ers that cover the roof,
making it difficult to
determine where the
ground ends and the
roof begins. Creating this
way of living has a posi-
tive influence not just on
the people in the neigh-
borhood but on the
entire ecosystem.
Gernot's research and
dedication to sustainable
living is the reason earth
construction and green
roofs have grown to
their current level of
popularity throughout
Germany. I've found a
meadow, a bit of country
in the city, and it's up on
Gernot's roof.

His present home sits in an area that was once considered undesirable because of its proximity to small industry, so the city easily supported the greening of the neighborhood. The community is a model for ecological development, and Gernot is the founder and mastermind of the project. Building codes require that the homes have a grass roof, only natural landscape barriers be constructed (no fences are allowed), roads remain unsealed so rain doesn't run off, and cars be parked in an area away from the houses. The result is a lush oasis in the middle of suburbia. The housing development is hardly discernable from a distance.

∧ (top left) GERNOT'S CASUAL LIVING ROOM OFFERS A BUILT-IN, COZY SEATING NICHE. THE CIRCULAR ARRANGEMENT OF THE DOMES CREATES INTIMATE AND HARMONIOUS LIVING SPACES.

∧ (top right) THE KITCHEN DOME.

< ALL THE ROOMS MOVE OUT FROM THIS CENTRAL DOME. THE VAST SPACE ABOVE MAKES THIS FEEL LIKE A MUCH LARGER ROOM.

After all the science of building, Gernot's art of clay construction takes on a new meaning in his bathroom and sunroom. Imagine doing pottery using coiled construction. Then think of the size of a room, and you have the technique that snakes around the room and forms the unusual look in the bathroom (including the clay sink) and the walls in the sunroom. Beyond his artistic building, Gernot finds time to oil paint. Inspired from dream images and influenced by themes in Native American art, abstract painting is his other creative passion. His paintings grace the walls of clay throughout the house, adding a colorful and spiritual dimension.

When he isn't teaching at the university, Gernot works in his office and studio at home. One of the connecting domes houses his architecture business where plans for new clay construction buildings are in progress. Recently completed is a 36-foot (11-meter) dome kindergarten with an acoustic adobe brick construction. Teachers marvel at the unique feeling and sound the structure provides.

Gernot wanted to live in a dome. He says, "The connection to the sky within the dome is inspirational. It also gives me a feeling of

< THE SUNROOM OPENS TO THE BACK GARDEN. THE UNASSUM-ING EXTERIOR IS ALL PART OF THE ATTRACTION TO CREATING A HOME THAT SO PERFECTLY FITS ITS ENVIRONMENT.

> THE SUNROOM IS FILLED WITH LIGHT ALL DAY AND LEADS TO THE BACK GARDEN. THE ROOM FEATURES TWO DIFFERENT STYLES OF CLAYWORK—THE COILS AND THE DAUBS OF MUD.

peace and security." Walking from the central dome into another, you sense a natural flow and movement. The soft light from above provides the very feeling Gernot wanted to achieve. With the construction of his home, Gernot has created a model for other earthen homes. People travel from all over to visit his home and gain inspiration using this healthy and sustainable building method. The possibilities are endless for Gernot in the realm of clay construction. He continues to promote this style of living and the ecological, social, and health benefits through his teaching, workshops, and travels.

SANTA CRUZ
CERAMIC SYMPHONY

∧ MATTIE LEEDS AT WORK ON HIS WHEEL
IN HIS STUDIO.

> THIS HIGHLIGHTS A SMALL PORTION OF THE WALL
THAT EXTENDS AROUND THE PERIMETER OF THE
PROPERTY.

< THE GATE BECKONS YOU TO ENTER THE FANTASTIC
WORLD OF MATTIE AND HIS SCULPTURAL WALL.

➼ *I've sought out an artist in the Santa Cruz Mountains, who recommends I visit his neighbor, Mattie Leeds. I wander next door, hearing the melancholy sounds of an oboe drift through the air. Walking through the gate, I've entered another world as this sculptural, undulating wall draws me onward. Musical instruments, huge clay vessels, glass, and stone tumble around in a great wall, and I'm standing in awe when Mattie appears, oboe in hand, inquiring as to why I'm standing in his yard. Of course, it's obvious to me why someone would be dumbstruck in his yard, but I mumble my apologies and quickly tell him of my search for artists. He is interested in participating, but I'll have to come back after he's finished practicing. He encourages me to poke around and then retreats inside. The haunting oboe melody begins again as I plan my return.*

A 15-minute drive out of Santa Cruz, California, nestled in the redwood-covered hills, lies the rustic home of ceramist, sculptor, painter, and musician Mattie Leeds. The modest, woodsy house has the imprint of original style and true character, much like Mattie himself. The oversized fireplace fills the living room with warmth on those days when the damp fog rolls in from the coast just a few miles away. Mattie spends much of his time in the over 2,000-square-foot (186-square-meter) studio located adjacent to the house where he may have as many as three or four large ceramic vessels in progress at a time. A series of wheels to throw the pots and a kiln the size of

a small room are integral elements for producing his 5- and 6-foot-tall (1.5- to 1.8-meter-tall) pots. Figures dancing, playing instruments and circling the pots are painted in colorful scenes for the finale. The studio was the first building he constructed on the property when he moved there 20 years ago. Mattie lived in a trailer while he built the house. Over the years of living on the property, Mattie gradually came to the design of the house and placement on the lot. He built the house in stages, as money permitted. He started with the bathroom, then moved on to the kitchen, which took two years to complete. He says, "The creation of the house was a process that I was pregnant with. The house was very synchronistic. I was able to give my full attention to each thing I did." Mattie feels that his home and this special place in the mountains is "a stage for things to be created, but it's also about creating the stage."

➥ *Mattie is a gentle,
complex, and elfin char-
acter. He is enthusiastic
about this book, and the
creative ideas are flow-
ing. We've talked a little
about his portrait, and
after some thought he
excitedly approaches me.
"I've got a great idea!
How about you photo-
graph me inside my kiln
with it on while I'm playing the oboe." I wonder
to myself if I have
enough liability for such
a photo, know that I
don't, and say, "Perfect!
Let's do it."*

*That's just the kind of
spark I have come to see
is part of Mattie's daily
life. As I move about his
world and my camera
comes in close, the artistic mystery he's created
up here is what I love to
try to capture on film.*

Many hands were involved in the building process, but one craftsman and friend, Michael Eckerman, did all the stonework on the fireplace, chimney, and the great wall. Although Mattie conceived and designed everything, he credits Michael and their collaboration for the success of the project. They happened to be together on the day in 1989, when an earthquake hit the area. They returned to Mattie's shop and found all of his huge pots in pieces. That's when they decided to incorporate the broken pots into the wall and chimney. Mattie says, "It set us off into the flow."

The wall, gate, and hot tub are the elements of Mattie's world that define the exterior personality. Spending 10 years on one project involves a great deal of patience and faith that the end result will be a creative masterpiece. He and Michael would work on one section at a time for a

^ HIS LARGE BODY OF WORKS WAITING FOR THEIR NEXT HOME.

< (opposite, top) MATTIE WARMS UP ON HIS OBOE IN HIS ROOM-SIZED KILN.

< (opposite, bottom) THE CHARACTERS THAT DANCE AROUND MATTIE'S POTS COME TO LIFE AS TWILIGHT FALLS ON THIS WILD WOODLAND WORLD, WITH CHOP SUEY LIGHTING THE WAY.

➥ Finishing my day of photography, I reflect on the world that Mattie is creating in these wooded hills. Part flashback to the '60s, part Eastern influence, part California commune, and all original, this place is uniquely Mattie. There is so much to take in at Mattie's place, but I never felt overwhelmed. That is also Mattie in a nutshell. He's a lively character with many layers of artistic talent and a personality that is contemplative, funny, full of surprises, and never too serious. Mattie carries the attitude of possibility and truly believes that "the world will provide if you can just dream." As I head down the mountain, I know that Mattie's vivid dreams will continue to manifest in a colorful and spirited way at his Chop Suey retreat.

few months, then take some time off, which allowed for renewed interest and ideas to evolve. Although there are individual vignettes and areas of interest, the wall flows as one piece. The wall includes musical instruments, hand-blown glass, statues, toys, Mattie's large vessels buried in the wall creating small caves, an antique wood stove, ceramic sculptures, plates, and virtually anything else that has inspired Mattie, and all based in Michael's creative stonework. The large Chop Suey sign came from a restaurant in San Francisco's Chinatown that was closing. The mosaic hot tub was the last addition. His large pots tumble water into each other, creating an inviting waterfall and a watery haven for a relaxing soak. Mattie says, "Having the philosophy that you're only limited by your own mind is critical to creating."

It is just that way of thinking that brought Mattie to music and his oboe. He was in his early 40s when he was encouraged to pick up the oboe. He has occasionally played with the Santa Cruz Community Orchestra and has found another creative outlet, both in his music and making the reeds for his playing.

Mattie is a constant stream of artistic expression. He is always grateful for the teachers that have given so much, especially the belief in himself that he can do whatever he was inspired to do. He's talking of a friend moving a piano to the house, which may mean building an addition. He says, "I want this to be a place where people come and share with me. It isn't just for me." He adds hopefully, "If I can just touch a few people to where they feel they could throw big pots or paint or play music, then I've succeeded."

< (opposite) MATTIE'S ARTISTIC AND SPIRITUAL LIFE IS INFLU-
ENCED BY ASIAN CULTURE, AND IT'S EVIDENT THROUGHOUT
THE PROPERTY AND IN HIS WORK. THE CHOP SUEY SIGN WAS
A FIND FROM A RESTAURANT THAT WAS GOING OUT OF BUSI-
NESS IN SAN FRANCISCO. THE POT THAT SEEMS TO OVER-
HANG AND SHOOT OUT OF THE WALL IS FILLED WITH EVERY-
THING FROM TOOLS TO HAND-BLOWN GLASS AND CERAMICS.

> (top) MATTIE CREATED A WATERFALL FROM SEVERAL OF HIS
LARGE VESSELS, WHICH RECYCLES THE WATER AND SPILLS
INTO EACH OTHER. WHEN SITTING IN THE LARGE MOSAIC HOT
TUB, THE WATERFALL PROVIDES REFRESHING SPLASHES OF
COOL WATER.

> (bottom) THE WALL CONTAINS MANY OBJECTS OF INTEREST
BEYOND CERAMICS AND STONE. MATTIE'S PASSION FOR
MUSIC IS REFLECTED IN MANY AREAS OF THE WALL, INCLUD-
ING FRENCH HORNS AND THIS SAXOPHONE, WHICH SPEWS
MORE THAN MUSIC.

COLORFUL
MAINE COTTAGE

< (far left) PORTRAIT OF CAROL BASS ON HER FRONT PORCH.

< CAROL'S DISTINCTLY VINTAGE-FEELING FABRIC COVERS HER BIG CHAIRS THAT HUG THE CONCRETE FIREPLACE.

^ CAROL'S COLORFUL OILS AND A SCULPTURE FROM HER SERIES "WALKING HOUSE" GREET VISITORS IN HER ENTRY HALL.

➥ *It's a short drive from
the thriving harbor city
of Portland, Maine, to
Carol Bass's island home,
but it seems worlds
away. The drive over
bridges and across
waterways is quintessen-
tially Maine. Tucked in
the thick birch woods, it's
hard to find the house
that Carol calls home.
The dark green exterior
and the log accents make
it almost invisible in the
forest. I'm wondering
what could be behind
the big windows that
more than one person
has said is truly an
artist's home.*

Carol Bass loves her bike rides on the coastal roads of Maine. Always keeping an eye out for the island property where she could build her home, she fell in love with this wooded lot. It was years in the making, but in 1999, the house she designed with her former husband came to fruition. Island living is important to her. It's surrounded by nature, a refuge from the city, and yet close enough to take advantage of all that the city offers.

Carol has a long history of design, so the creation of her house came naturally. She is the cofounder of Maine Cottage Furniture, a popular line of contemporary furniture. The company started as a result of Carol's yearning to find colorful furniture that didn't interfere with contemporary art, but at the same time had a distinctly New England flavor. She comments, "You couldn't go anywhere and find, for example, a pink dresser." In true entrepreneurial spirit, she and her husband started the furniture line in 1988, and it has become a thriving business.

Carol graduated from the University of Georgia with a bachelor's degree in fine arts. Oil painting has always been her love, and now she devotes herself full-time to her painting career, stepping away from the furniture business. Even so, her house design, the colors, the furniture, and the art that fill it are very much a part of her creating. She says, "It's most important to learn who you are so you can sincerely, really sincerely, express yourself in your home so that it will be only you. I feel a great deal of sadness for people constructing these large homes and doing only what is the latest trend or what the magazines tell them to do. They are really missing part of the scenery on the journey."

> (opposite, top) THE LIVING ROOM IS AWASH WITH BRIGHT COLORS, INCLUDING HER LINE OF FURNITURE. THE LOG POSTS ARE MADE FROM BIRCH TREES HARVESTED FROM HER LAND WHEN THE EXCAVATION OCCURRED.

> (opposite, bottom) THE MAINE COTTAGE FURNITURE CHAIR IS TUCKED IN THE CORNER OF THE LIVING ROOM WITH HER SCULPTURES AND THE VIEW OF THE BIRCH FOREST OUTSIDE.

Carol is busy preparing for a gallery show on our day of photography, so I am working on my own, enjoying the quiet woods that surround the house and the doors that open to the outside. The house is a bright and colorful contrast to a typical New England house. It's a bit of Caribbean island colors meets the Maine woods, and the effect is uplifting and spirited. That is something that comes up often for Carol when she talks about home—the spirit of the home, how to achieve it, and the way we can find the spirit in our own dwellings.

➥ As I make my way off the island, I'm reflecting on the colorful cottage and the wonderful composition of furniture, color, materials, and light. Carol has artfully achieved an inviting and lively home, a playful sanctuary. I feel energized after spending a day there and know her influence will reach my home in Colorado. Carol says, "My whole life is about trying to find my home." I know what she refers to is more a spiritual home than a physical home, but it is the physical home that can support the search. Carol has come very close to finding that home and it's on the other side of the bridge I've just crossed on my journey to wonderful artists' homes.

Sticks and twigs speak to Carol. The large log posts used throughout are birch logs that came from the property when they cleared for the foundation. Carol speaks with a reverence for the sticks that she considers the bones of the house. Her sculpture series of "Walking Houses" is composed of wood that she finds on the island shores. She says, "I like thinking, 'Here is this beautiful wood, it's a connection to the home and the materials, to the bones of our houses, to our bones.'" Her Walking Houses are symbols of the journey the houses want to take and the journey you make together. She believes, "Your house is alive, and you should show that aliveness in your home."

Concrete and wooden floors, contemporary lighting, and large picture windows that open to the woods on all sides are some of the other bones that make up the home. She used antique doors in many of the rooms to give the house a little history. The bold colors she used are a match for her furniture designs and complement her vivacious personality and artistic style. Carol's studio is located at one end of the home, and the glass doors separating her studio from the living area provide a quiet work space. Her oil paintings, her mixed-media sculptures, and the work of other artists are displayed throughout the house. Many of her oil paintings explore the subjects of home and place. Although she draws her inspiration from the time she spends in nature, she doesn't paint it. She uses lots of color and works in a primitive style that she partially attributes to her southern upbringing.

Carol is very clear about her intentions for her home. She says, "When someone enters my home, I want them to feel that they can jump off into a world just beneath the surface and catch a slipstream of sorts—a world where color ignites passion and possibility not considered before. I want guests to feel the zestful spirit that living with art can bring. I wish for all to understand that home life should not be lived as if it were for resale."

Carol's home is a direct influence on her art, and her art is strongly influenced by her surroundings. The two aspects of her life are always intertwined, each always reflecting the other. The explorations of houses as a theme in her art and the ongoing relationship with her home are a vital source of creativity. The design and evolution of her home is a delightful parallel to the journey she continues with art. As her "Walking House" series depicts, it's a journey that artist and home walk together.

∧ (above) THE LONG DINING-ROOM TABLE MADE FROM TWO SPLIT LOGS IS PERFECT FOR A LARGE CROWD.

< (left) CAROL'S PASSION FOR THE DRIFTWOOD ON THE ISLAND IS SHOWCASED IN THE DESIGN OF HER STAIRS. SHE CALLS THE STICKS THE "BONES" OF THE HOUSE.

< (opposite) CAROL'S COUNTRY-FEELING KITCHEN IS FILLED WITH MODERN CONVENIENCES, USES CONTEMPORARY MATERIALS, SUCH AS THESE CONCRETE COUNTERTOPS, AND IS FILLED WITH BRIGHT SHADES OF VINTAGE POTTERY.

LITTLE HAVANA HACIENDAS

∧ A COLLECTION OF GLASS OBJECTS IN PABLO'S WINDOW.
PABLO SAYS, "ARTISTS ARE MIRRORS REFLECTING
EVERYTHING AROUND THEM—DIFFERENT FACETS THAT
BECOME ONE."

> PABLO'S GARDEN IS FULL OF HIS ANIMATED
SCULPTURES OF SCRAP METALS AND FOUND PARTS.

< PORTRAIT OF PABLO CANO, HIS MOTHER, MARGARITA, AND HIS FATHER, PABLO SENIOR.

∨ INSIDE PABLO'S HOME IS A WORK IN PROGRESS— HIS LIFE-SIZED SCULPTURE MARIONETTES, WHICH WILL BECOME PART OF A THEATRICAL PRODUCTION.

Miami is new territory for me, and I come with all kinds of exotic notions of a city rich in cultural diversity, steamy nights by the ocean, and sensual Cuban-influenced music drifting through the neighborhoods. Tapping into the Cuban community and art scene is of primary interest to me because I feel it may be at the heart of Miami culture. When I meet artist Pablo Cano, my instincts are confirmed. I am drawn into his world in Little Havana and will later meet his family, who will broaden my perspective and show me the side of Miami I had hoped to find.

In this quiet neighborhood is the rather modest home of Pablo Cano. What lies inside is a quirky launch pad for mixed-media assemblages. Life-sized marionettes of found objects constitute his current series of work. The final product is a cast of characters for stage performances, involving everything from set designs to soundtracks for his sculpted marionettes.

After graduating from Queens College in New York City and getting his master's degree in fine arts, he traveled and studied in Europe. He returned home to Miami and became an adjunct professor at New World School of Arts. He knew he had reached a certain level of success as an artist when he was able, with the support of his family, to purchase his home in 1989. Pablo says, "My home has to be a sanctuary. How else can I work?" The little haven he has created is a testament to his visual journey.

Outside, his gardens are full of his fanciful, figurative sculptures. Made from car parts, scrap metal, old patio furniture, and other interesting objects he finds, these sculptures have a distinctly old-world feeling, despite the contemporary materials. Pablo has a natural affinity for the garden, which he attributes to his mother's influence.

∧ (above) DETAIL OF MARGARITA'S PAINTINGS OF SAINTS AND CUBAN WOMEN RAFTING TO FREEDOM.

< (opposite) PABLO'S BEDROOM.

Talking about living in Little Havana can't be done without mentioning Pablo's family. Art runs deep in the family, from his mother's folk art depicting the raft rides from Cuba to freedom, to the music of his father and his recording studio—the first Cuban-owned studio in Miami. When Pablo needs help for the soundtrack on his productions, he commissions one of the best in the business, his father. Pablo senior's music-recording business is renowned in Miami. Working with the likes of Arturo Sandoval and Tito Puente, he put Cuban musicians on the American map. His sister, Isabel Hernandez, takes after dad in that music is her calling. She is an accomplished guitarist and has received a bachelor's degree in piano from Florida International University.

➥ On this hot Miami morning, Pablo and I are sitting in his garden sipping thick Cuban coffee and talking about his art. He's excited about the show that's opening at the New World Gallery in Miami of his animated, life-sized marionettes. He suggests we take a drive to have a look, and then go visit his parents. As the day unfolds I have not only been warmly welcomed by Pablo but captivated by his mother and father, their flight from Cuba in 1962, and their many artistic and intellectual pursuits.

Pablo's mother, Margarita Cano, is an accomplished woman, especially in the realm of education and the arts. Growing up in Cuba, her formal education in Havana included a doctorate in physics and chemistry. When the revolution began, she started working in the Havana Library and pursued a degree in library science. After enduring hardships under Castro and watching censorship affect her library, the family immigrated to the United States, just four days before the Cuban Missile Crisis in 1962. Soon after, Margarita, Pablo senior, and their two children arrived in Miami, and she began her work at the Miami-Dade Library as the art librarian. In 1972, she established the program for a permanent collection of fine art at the Miami-Dade County Library. She sought funding and grant money and curated a world-class collection of fine art. The fact that she speaks three languages and has her doctorate made her indispensable to the growing library.

Margarita's childhood was filled with a plethora of international influences, including intellectuals and scientists from Russia and Germany. Although her father was a stout atheist and her upbringing included more science than religion, her first paintings as a child contained the image of Madonna and child. Her paintings always depict angels, saints, and the bereft mother and child on their float to freedom. After raising her family and retiring from the library in 1993, she was able to once again resume her painting. She was given a show of her work at the Gallery of the Eccentric in Miami, and her art began again in earnest. She paints small boxes, canvases, and thought-filled books with paintings and inspirational text. The romantic quality of Margarita's paintings belies the hardship that the Cuban immigrants must face.

146

➥ *Margarita and Pablo treat me to lunch at one of their favorite Cuban cafés. This is the kind of day that reminds me of why I began photographing artists and their homes. It's a completely fulfilling journey where I'm given a brief glimpse into the ways creativity and diverse backgrounds influence how people live. From one day to the next, I gain not only this broader vision and understanding but also friends in cities that yesterday were foreign to me.*

∧ (above) MARGARITA AND PABLO SENIOR'S LIVING ROOM IS FULL OF ART AND COLLECTIBLES THAT REMIND THEM OF THEIR LIFE IN CUBA. PABLO'S SCULPTURE SERVES AS A FIREPLACE ADORNMENT.

< (opposite) THE DINING AREA, WITH MARGARITA'S PAINTINGS ON THE WALL AND PABLO'S CERAMIC VESSEL ON THE TABLE.

Margarita and Pablo senior were great collectors of art in Cuba, which they unfortunately had to leave behind. Margarita swore she would not end up with things she would hate to part with, but the house they bought with just a few thousand dollars 40 years ago is now filled with Pablo's paintings, Margarita's colorful images, and many antiques and furniture that remind Margarita of her Cuban heritage. The dark wood and high ceilings have a distinctly Spanish influence. Her garden is a jungle of tropical plants and a retreat from the bustling neighborhood. As many were fleeing to the suburbs, the Cano family grew roots in this house in Little Havana. Pablo reflects, "It's important to honor the things about our home, our sanctuary, that we may take for granted. Even passing through a doorway has a trickle-down affect." The Cano family has an appreciation for their home and life in Little Havana that reaches beyond the experiences of most American citizens, one that comes from survival, perseverance, and a rich life that is full of art, education, music, and a passionate devotion to their family.

FRIENDS AND A FRENCH FLAT

∧ MONIQUE DRAI AND LOUISE GHIO IN THEIR
PARISIAN FLAT.

> THE MAGNIFICENT VIEW OF THE ARRONDISSEMENT,
OR DISTRICT, OF PARIS FROM THEIR ROSE-COVERED
BALCONY.

➥ *Springtime in Paris!
The roses that spill off
Monique and Louise's
balcony are in full
bloom. Songs have been
written about days like
this. Being in Paris photographing Monique and
Louise's chic apartment
seems to accentuate the
romance I feel for the
day. The vintage-style
flat coupled with effer-
vescent personalities
make this visit especially
fun for me. Our language
skills are limited only by
our degree of reserve,
and somehow we've
checked that at the door,
so our time together is
more than animated.*

The home inhabited by friends Louise Ghio and Monique Drai is located in a quintessential Parisian neighborhood. The views down the street of classic architecture and row houses are like a set from a movie. Mention movies and Louise perks up, as that is her current area of interest. Producing photography and films are the latest in many creative endeavors that Louise is pursuing. Monique is influenced by the history of the neighborhood as a leather manufacturing area and designs and produces her own line of leather handbags. She also sculpts in her free time.

When the time came to find the suitable place to live and work, Louise and Monique pooled their resources and got this apartment.

Although they like many different things, their interior design tastes run in a similar vein, so there is very little debate between the two as to how to furnish or what collectibles work together. The unique blend of '50s kitsch and '20s antiques seems the perfect complement to the turn-of-the-century building.

They like the unusual objects, ones that have a luxurious quality, but as Louise says, "We're not afraid of bad taste." Artfully combining objects from different eras with an eye to composition is the gift that Louise and Monique share. Their antique rugs and the '50s lamps work in harmony together.

^ (top left) THE ARCHITECTURAL ELEMENTS ATTRACTED MONIQUE AND LOUISE TO THIS FLAT, IN PARTICULAR THE DETAILING OF THE *CHEMINÉES*, OR FIREPLACE.

^ (top right) THE ECLECTIC VIGNETTE OF '50S LIGHTING, AN EGYPTIAN STATUE, BLACK-AND-WHITE PRINTS, AND AN OLD IRON BENCH SET THE TONE FOR THEIR STYLISH DECOR.

< (opposite) THIS VINTAGE LAMP, MADE FROM AN OSTRICH EGG, IS SURROUNDED BY OTHER COLLECTIBLES.

●◇ *My Parisian friend
and guide, Antonia, helps
us through difficult
translations for my inter-
view. Before long we are
all laughing and enjoying
each other's company. So
many times I'm asked if
understanding the lan-
guage is a problem in my
travels, but where there
is kindness and patience,
even in the most difficult
translations, there is
usually understanding.
With creative spirits like
Monique and Louise,
finding the common
ground to explore is a
pleasure.*

Louise and Monique came to this area about three years ago. They were immediately drawn to this neighborhood and, in particular, this apartment. Each room offered different design opportunities and plenty of room for each of them to have her own space. They loved the style of this apartment, which included architectural features such as a fireplace and floor-to-ceiling windows. They also knew the character of the flat would complement their eclectic furnishings.

After years of collecting they have decided to put their talented eyes to work and have opened a store of collectibles, featuring just the kind of style that is a trademark of their own apartment. The small shop, Les Trottoirs de Chanzy, in the Bastille district features European and American functional pieces and *objets d'arts* from the mid-19th century and the 1920s, '50s, and '70s. The shop reflects a range of years as diverse as their combined tastes.

Louise and Monique have created a life style together as only good friends can. They share a unique Parisian apartment where their decor expresses their combined tastes, partner in a business that evolved from a shared passion of collecting, and still pursue their individual art and design projects. When I asked them how they managed to keep it all together, Monique says, "We often like different things, but mostly it's all about good communication."

At the end of the day Antonia helps me down the flight of stairs with my equipment. She has introduced me to some of her finest friends and artists in Paris and shared with me an intimate look inside her circle in Paris. Her friends, Louise and Monique, graciously shared their home and the unique way they have created a style—and a business—together. I'm quite sure that when I return to Paris I'll have three more friends to call on.

< (top) THE SUNNY LIVING ROOM PROVIDES AN OPULENT BUT FUNKY ATMOSPHERE. MANY OF THEIR FAVORITE '50S LIGHT FIXTURES FILL THE ROOM WITH LIGHT.

< (bottom) SHEER BURGUNDY DRAPES CAST A WARM GLOW ON THE COZY DINING AREA.

BAYSIDE BARN

∧ ARTIST CRAIGIE SUCCOP IN HER CONVERTED
BARN-TURNED-STUDIO

> THE MOSAIC DESIGNS THAT GREET VISITORS AT
THE FRONT DOOR FEATURE THE PROPERTY'S
NAMESAKE, A TURTLE.

^ THE GLOW FROM CRAIGIE'S MOSAIC WINDOWS BY HER FRONT DOOR IS BEST SEEN AT TWILIGHT. THE GARDEN AND SCULPTURES HAVE SPECIAL ACCENT LIGHTING THAT MAKES THIS TIME IN THE GARDEN MAGICAL. MUCH OF THE DESIGN AND PLANTING OF THE GARDEN HAPPENED WITH THE HELP OF HER FRIEND, JULIE LOWE.

< THE FOUNTAIN WAS MADE FROM A FOUND CERAMIC ELECTRICAL PART WITH A BASIN THAT CRAIGIE TILED.

Craigie Succop's work as a fine artist began in earnest when she purchased her dream home, formerly a pig barn, near St Michaels, Maryland. It takes a certain kind of vision to take a barn and turn it into a pretty home. Although the former owners had worked to make the barn a summer home, it was Craigie's vision that transformed the building. She has made this old structure into a delightful bayside home. Craigie knew that the other large barn on the property would become her studio, and she set about making the changes necessary to remodel the home and turn the barn into a working studio.

Craigie's talent for decorating comes from a long history of working in design. She installed a new kitchen, put in new windows, and turned the sun porch into a year-round room. The original brick floors stayed. The home is surrounded on three sides by water, so when she approached the design of the sunroom, she wanted it to embrace the bay views. The large mosaic window that stretches the length of the sunroom is the focal point in the room, depicting the four seasons.

< (top) CRAIGIE'S CAT ENJOYS THE COLORFUL BEDROOM.

< (bottom left) THE FIREPLACE, CHAIR, SCULPTURES, AND TABLE ARE ALL EXAMPLES OF CRAIGIE'S ARTISTRY. THE STRIKING BLACK-AND-WHITE DECOR WITH ACCENTS OF RED ADDS TO THE DRAMA OF HER SETTING.

< (bottom right) WHAT WAS FORMERLY A PORCH, CRAIGIE CONVERTED TO A YEAR-ROUND ROOM. THE LARGE MOSAIC PANEL IS THE FOCAL POINT OF THE ROOM AND FEATURES THE FOUR SEASONS. WHEN IT COMES TO INSTALLING ANY SCULPTURES OR WINDOWS, CRAIGIE LOOKS TO HER NEIGHBOR AND FELLOW ARTIST MAC BUTTRILL FOR HELP.

➜ Upon arriving at the eastern shore of the Chesapeake Bay in Maryland, my first surprise is Craigie, the artist I've been e-mailing, is a woman, not a man. The next surprise is how charming the community of St. Michaels and the surrounding coastal habitat are. Egrets, herons, and osprey are a few of the birds that I encounter not five minutes into my visit. Winding my way down her road, I'm greeted by a colorful mosaic sign reading, "Turtle Cove," Craigie's aptly named property. Gardens begin at the driveway and don't stop until the water's edge. Coming from the arid Southwest, this humid, green haven washes over me, and I'm taken in by the bucolic scene before me.

Everything is considered a potential mosaic project at Turtle Cove. She laid smooth, round stones around the hearth of the fireplace, and all the windows are topped with one of her colorful mosaic valance designs. Tables, chairs, countertops, and bathtubs are covered in mosaic. There is no place where Craigie's creative hand hasn't been. Her friends tease, "If you stand still long enough, Craigie will mosaic you."

The natural world plays a large part in Craigie's life. Her artistic endeavors carry over into the garden and pool she designed and built. A mosaic whale swims along the edge of the pool, and sculptures fill the garden outside her front door. The fluid forms in many sizes of mosaic sculpture are placed throughout the grounds. Covered in rich colors and textured stones, they are the main attraction in the gardens.

There is little separation between the indoors and outdoors at Turtle Cove. The house seems to spill out into the garden, and the mosaic inlays in the sidewalk draw you back inside. The many outdoor rooms, pool house, fountains, and resting spots outside, along with the mild year-round climate, mean many hours are passed enjoying the gardens.

Craigie believes that eliminating from one's vocabulary the statement, "I'm not creative," or "I don't have any talent," is imperative to creating an inspired environment. Whether it's cooking, gardening, or painting, they are all artistic expressions. When people come to visit Craigie, she says, "I want them to come back again and again to see what's new or what I am working on. I want to create the unexpected but not works that are garish or full of controversy. I want visitors to feel the elements of serenity, introspection, and fantasy along with the unexpected, and I want them to relish in the privacy and peacefulness I have created here."

If Craigie has any regrets, it's that she didn't get started doing the art she loves so much at an earlier age. Seeing all that she has done to develop the world of Turtle Cove, it's clear that working double-time is nothing but a pleasure for her. Certainly the creative energy that she both gives to her life and gets from the environment is a symbiotic relationship that will only continue to grow.

∧ (left) CRAIGIE'S BLUE PATIO SETTING FEATURES HER BOLD MOSAIC AS A BACKDROP.

∧ (right) CRAIGIE COMPLETELY REMODELED THE KITCHEN AND, OF COURSE, ADDED MANY CREATIVE TOUCHES. THE MOSAIC VALENCES SHED BRILLIANT COLORED LIGHT ON THE ROOM. EVERY WINDOW FEATURES A DIFFERENT VARIATION OF THESE LIGHT-CATCHING ACCENTS.

➼ *Saying my goodbyes to Craigie is like leaving an old friend. I know I'll come back when I need a retreat from the hectic world and a warm welcome. I'm hoping that I'll get back here soon because I'm pretty sure Craigie won't be coming to visit me. And why would she want to go anywhere when the home and surroundings she's worked so hard to create offer the best rewards possible—peace, inspiration, and beauty.*

MOSTLY RED
AMSTERDAM
RETREAT

^ PORTRAIT OF PRINTMAKER KATE WILKINSON.

> FEARLESS COLOR AND COMPOSITION RULE
  IN KATE'S TINY APARTMENT.

Kate Wilkinson came to Amsterdam from her native England. She graduated from Hull College of Art in East Yorkshire, England, during which time she did an art exchange to Holland. Fourteen years later, she still makes Holland her home. She likens Amsterdam to a world village that is vibrant and people friendly. Visually, she is attracted to what she calls, "the horizontal lines of Holland's landscape." Kate is best known for her screen printing and monoprints. "I like the printing process because of the placement of things and layering. I also like the mechanical and labor-intensive aspects involved in printing," she says. Her collage-like images are full of memories of travel and American icons. Her recent pieces were especially influenced by her trip to the American Southwest.

It seems natural that her little place on the top floor of her building would be as lively and colorful as her work. However, you won't see much of her art on the walls because, she says, "I wanted to create

a haven, even a haven from my work. I make a conscious effort to create a separate space for living." She works in her studio, a quick bicycle ride away, so she can come home and leave the work behind.

Kate's fourth-floor apartment is located in one of the classic Canal District row houses. Old and slightly worn, the addition of paint and a lot of ingenuity gave this otherwise run-down, two-room flat a fabulous face-lift. Kate loves color. She says, "The oranges and reds make me feel luxurious and warm. You can't be colorful enough."

^ (top left) KATE'S UNDERSTATED COLLECTION OF OBJECTS IS EVIDENT IN THIS CORNER. THE "G" SHE FOUND IN A DUMPSTER.

^ (top right) ATTENTION TO DETAIL, FROM THE FLOWERS TO THE POLKA-DOT PITCHER, ALL FITS IN HER RED-AND-BLUE FLAT.

< (opposite) THE CATS REST EASILY IN THE WARM RED ROOM.

I've quickly learned that everyone in Amsterdam lives at the top of the narrowest stairs possible. Kate's apartment is no exception, and after four flights of hauling my bags up and feeling certain I was going to fall backward, I have arrived. I set my bags down only to discover the front of my shirt is covered with what I had unknowingly rolled the wheels of my expensive camera bag through—something all too common on the sidewalks in Amsterdam. Kate laughs and says, "The Dutch consider that good luck!" as she hustles me to the sink to try to wash the smelly deposit off my shirt. Although I'm slightly embarrassed, it just takes a short time before I've forgotten my entrance and I'm comfortable in Kate's red world.

∧ THE SMALL BALCONY GARDEN OFFERS REFUGE FROM THE BUSTLING STREET AS WELL AS A QUIET DINING SPOT.

> (opposite) KATE'S DINING ROOM.

Add collectibles, sometimes even throwaway stuff Kate has found, and lots of color, and you have the beginning of her decorating formula. She says, "My life is a collage, so my world reflects that. The juxtaposition of colors and objects may mean very different things in a new context." Although she loves to collect, she's says, "Possessions really don't have much meaning, and if I lost it all, it's all stuff that could go." Perhaps that is what gives her a fearless approach to her retreat.

Like so many artists, Kate encourages others to look within and "be brave." She calls her process, "Yoga for the brain." Taking this little place and turning it into a gem took neither lots of money nor lots of resources, just a little of what seems to come to Kate so easily— courage and creativity.

➡ *Something that my travel to artists' homes is showing me is that it can take as much or as little as you want to put into it to create your look. Kate is an example of how paint and found objects define her style. Sometimes, just following a funny idea can lead to a design statement. Allowing those ideas to surface and encourage thinking beyond the concept of buying the latest style of couch or following the current trend is what artists like Kate have perfected. Perhaps it's having limited financial resources, but I think it's more about thinking that finances don't have to be a limitation to getting the creative juices flowing. As I plunge down the stairs, and Kate and I have a cup of tea at her favorite café, I'm thinking of my own small house and all I can do with as little or as much as I choose.*

TROMPE L'OEIL
IN TANDEM

∧ PORTRAIT OF CHRISTINE AND JEFFREY CROZIER ON THEIR
PATIO IN CALIFORNIA WITH A TUSCAN BACKDROP.

> THE INSPIRED TRANSFORMATION OF AN OTHERWISE DRAB
ASSISTED-LIVING FACILITY DINING ROOM WAS ACHIEVED BY
CHRISTINE'S AND JEFFREY'S *TROMPE L'OEIL* TALENTS.

When I first met Chris and Jeff, I was enchanted by how thoroughly their lives reflected art. I know of no one quite like them. Chris can whip up scones for breakfast, paint an oil still life in the morning, take a break to sing a selection from the musical Les Miserables with Jeff masterfully accompanying her on the piano, and have a five-course meal, using vegetables from their garden, prepared for 10 friends by 6:00 P.M. And this is no exaggeration! They live and breathe art, from culinary creations to music and painting. There have been no finer moments, or meals, than those I've shared at their dinner table, which is another display of Christine's painting talent, featuring a trompe l'oeil scene to whet the appetite.

Christine and Jeffrey Crozier's homes are a perfect example of blending art into everyday living. The magic of their brush strokes transforms their somewhat ordinary tract home in Santa Fe, New Mexico, and their small Victorian in Pacific Grove, California, into a gallery of color, sophistication, and harmony. Their talent spans the realms of decorating walls of some of America's most famous homes and creating murals and healing environments in hospitals to painting *plein-air* oil landscapes in the arroyos and mesas surrounding Santa Fe and the seashore of Carmel. Chris says, "I've reached a place where I don't believe that my art and my life are separate. They're completely integrated. If I take a day off, I either will cook, which is a manipulation of materials; garden, which is also a manipulation of materials, texture, and colors; or paint. There are similarities between all these processes."

< (opposite) IT'S HARD TO TELL WHAT IS REAL AND WHAT IS ILLUSION IN THE DINING ROOM. THE FLORA MOVES FROM THE DINING TABLE TO THE WALLS, CREATING AN ENCHANTING ENVIRONMENT.

> (right) THE KITCHEN OF THEIR SANTA FE HOME HAD ORDINARY PAINTED CABINETS. THEY PAINTED THEM IN A FAUX CHERRY WOOD ON THE TRIM AND PAINTED THE FASCIAS TO LOOK LIKE PUNCHED TIN.

↪ Coming to visit in Santa Fe or California, I'm always ready to spend some time under the roof that is one of their canvases—perhaps it's the gourmet meals I devour or the walks on the beach a few blocks away, but most likely it's the embrace of my friends and the lively activities we're sure to find together. Today as we're photographing the Tuscan scene on their patio, the entire neighborhood is coming to find out what we're up to, because they know all too well there is always something going on at the Croziers'.

Their home in the heart of Santa Fe is a reflection of their talents in all areas. The Croziers' hacienda is warmed by a four-color glaze on the walls in the living room, recreating the rich adobe walls of the past. The simple kitchen cabinets that came with the house were transformed to fool even the most discerning eye. Faux cherrywood grain is painted on the trim, whereas the fascias are painted to look like punched tin. Their dining room is graced with a plethora of foliage and flora. Pomegranates and pears spill off the walls, and sparrows and swallows dance around the ceiling. Christine says, "It hasn't always been a popular concept in art that beauty is important, but I do believe it is important to live our lives in beauty, whether it is painting or the way I do my house or the way I think about things as I go about my day. I want to approach life with grace and beauty."

Decorative art is one way that Jeff fills his life with beauty. "I think we, as a society, need to honor our living spaces and recognize them as sanctuaries. By creating an environment that is filled with beauty, we are nurtured in all areas of life. Our home is a reflection of us and expresses our inner being. We want guests to be able to walk into our home and know that they're in a place of nurturing." The art of creating their home is an ongoing process. "It's never quite finished, or rather, there are always new paintings and ideas to work on. It's not the end product but the process we're interested in," says Jeff.

Christine's focus with her art career is her *plein-air* oil painting. Both she and Jeff tote their easels filled with oils around the world and can quickly capture the feeling and essence of any landscape or cityscape. Their paintings of Tuscan villages in Italy; lush, tropical beaches in Fiji; or the foggy coast of Carmel are all rich and dramatically rendered with broad, colorful brush strokes.

➡ I am fortunate that Chris and Jeff are two of my dearest friends. Always fearless, they forge ahead in the true artists' way. They have formed a unique and lasting partnership. Their lives and talents are infectious; their love is genuine. They are talented teachers and eager students, a rich combination that is unmatched in my world. Their influence reaches deep in my life, and their encouragement on my own artistic path is priceless. The path of living beauty in every moment with every task they tackle is a special gift they share with all who come in contact with them.

< (top) THE BEDROOM OF THE PACIFIC GROVE HOUSE HAS A THREE-COLOR GLAZE WITH A BAMBOO TRELLIS PAINTED ON THE LIGHTLY CLOUDY CEILING.

< (bottom) JEFFREY'S PIANO SITS IN FRONT OF A WALL OF CHRISTINE'S OIL PAINTINGS.

ABOUT THE AUTHOR

Laurie E. Dickson is a photographer based out of Durango, Colorado, and a regular contributor to shelter magazines around the world, including *Natural Home*, *Better Homes and Gardens* and their Special Interest Publications, *Sunset*, *Log Home Living*, and *Timber Frame Homes*. She's an avid gardener, skier, yogi, hiker, and world traveler, always in search of her next inspiring subject.

RESOURCES

THINKING BIG FIEBIG
Eberhard Fiebig
Hannoversche Str. 4
34346 Hann.munden
Germany
www.art-engineering.de

LIVING OUT LOUD
Kathleen Pearson
Bisbee, AZ
USA
☎ 520-432-5230
www.artcaragency.com
love23@theriver.com

HARBOR HIDEAWAY
Sarah Grierson-Irving
Mousehole, Penzance
Cornwall
UK
☎ (01736) 732062

JAZZY PARISIAN PAINTER
Françoise Biver
Paris
France
☎ 01-40-18-38-23

DIVINE DUMPSTER DECOR
Nancy Scott
Bisbee, AZ
USA
☎ 520-432-1789
bisbeerose@aol.com

Prana's Bistro and Hotel
Bisbee, AZ
USA
☎ 520-432-1832

SAN FRANCISCO CHIC
Silvia Poloto
San Francisco, CA
USA
silvia@poloto.com

Rugs from
www.returntotradition.com

Hang
Gallery 556
Sutter St.
San Francisco, CA 94102
USA
☎ 415-434-HANG
www.hangart.com

PEACEFUL SANTA FE PUEBLO
Estella Loretto
Santa Fe, NM
USA
☎ 505-986-8471
www.estellaloretto.com

FOREST ROOMS
Mary Ellen Long
Durango, CO
USA
wmelart@yahoo.com

Robischon Gallery
1740 Wazee St.
Denver, CO 80202
USA

Sears-Peyton Gallery
New York, NY
USA
searspeyt@aol.com

Architect Dean Brookie
1221 Main Ave.
Durango, CO 81301
USA

WEST PALM PARADISE
Bruce Helander
447 S. Rosemary Ave., Ste. 302
West Palm Beach, FL 33401
USA
☎ 561-655-0504
www.helander.biz

MANHATTAN VIEWS IN VIBRANT HUES
Apryl Miller
New York, NY
USA
Apryl26@hotmail.com

Rebecca Spivack
Venetian plaster
☎ 917-273-9259

HEAVENLY HAVEN
Alison Englefield and Clare Calder-Marshall
St. Just, Cornwall
UK
www.artwaves.co.uk
clare.calder-marshall@virgin.net

ODE TO SOUTHERN ROOTS
Willie Little
Charlotte, NC
USA
☎ 704-376-7864
www.willielittle.com

Noel Gallery
401 N. Tryon St., Ste. 104
Charlotte, NC 28202
USA
www.noelgallery.com

LUNA PARC
Ricky Boscarino
Sussex County, NJ
USA
☎ 973-948-2160

www.lunaparc.com

LOFTY BOSTON
Fort Point Channel
Boston, MA
USA
www.fortpointarts.org

Joanne Kaliontzi
Anthony Montalto, architect
jkali@aol.com

Dorothea Van Camp and
Jeffrey Heyne
www.unit35.com

Rob Reeps
robreeps@rcn.com

Marie Galvin
www.mariegalvindesigns.com

CORNISH COAST
GUARD COTTAGE
Peter Eveleigh
St. Levan, Penzance
Cornwall
UK
☎ (01736) 810571

CAROLINA COMTEMPORARY
Eric Anderson
Charlotte, NC
USA

Joie Lassiter Gallery
318 E. 9th St.
Charlotte, NC 28202
USA
☎ 704-373-1462
www.lassitergallery.com

GOING DUTCH
Marga Wurpel and Yvonne Piller
Santpoort
Netherlands

Hors Art, Santpoort
Netherlands
Horsart@xs4all.nl
Mwurpel@hetnet.nl
Yvonne.piller@xs4all.nl

MASTER IN MUD
Gernot Minke
Kassel
Germany
☎ 0561-883050
Feb@architektur.uni-kassel.de

The Earth Construction Handbook,
by Gernot Minke

SANTA CRUZ CERAMIC
SYMPHONY
Mattie Leeds
Santa Cruz, CA
USA
☎ 831-429-8123
mattieleeds@cruzio.com

COLORFUL MAINE COTTAGE
Carol Bass
Yarmouth, ME
USA
☎ 207-846-5414
cbass@maine.rr.com

LITTLE HAVANA HACIENDAS
The Cano Family, Pablo Cano
Miami, FL
USA
☎ 305-856-5031
www.canoart.com

DEDICATION

This book is dedicated to artist and friend Rachel Crossley.

It was with a tremendous sense of loss during the writing of the text that I learned of Rachel Crossley's passing. The car accident that took her life happened on the winding roads of Cornwall, not far from her home and her beloved Peter. Although my time with her was brief, her warmth and vitality lingered. She was a friend I'd hoped to see again. As I share the tales of artists' lives, the stories must someday cycle to their passing. Rachel's story continues in the memory and lives of those that knew and loved her.

ACKNOWLEDGMENTS

Heartfelt thank-yous to Angie and Peter Butler—for getting my European search off to a stellar start in Cornwall; Antonia Ceppi, my Parisian angel; Gernot Minke, for going out of his way to introduce me to Eberhard; my cousin Kirk and his family in Amsterdam; Joie and Michael Lassiter of Joie Lassiter Gallery, for their time and referrals in Charlotte, NC; Leah Edwards from Hang gallery in San Francisco; Joanne Kaliontzi, for turning me on to Fort Point in Boston; my Aunt Nancy, Uncle Don, and cousins, for their support in Maine; my sister, Julie, in Keene, NH; all the friends that put me up for a night and fed me while I visited in their neighborhoods; the Imagesmith in Durango, CO, for always getting the film right; my editor, Mary Ann Hall; my always encouraging photo editor, Betsy Gammons; my family, for supporting me, especially when my own home was threatened by forest fires; my friends Mary and Tony, who are always there for me; the artists I couldn't include—thanks for understanding—there may be another on the way; and, most of, all to the artists I did include, who opened their homes and hearts to inspire me and make my dream possible.